"In thirty years of pastoral ministry, I can't think of a single issue that has come up more in conversations with hurting people than the issue of forgiveness. In nearly every case, these people know they need to forgive. That part is clear. What is unclear is how. That's what sets this book apart from every other work I've read on the subject. This book is all about how—and I love that. Mark is just the man to help us navigate this. He lives what he writes, and I love that too. I predict you'll end up buying copies to give away."

Dr. Daniel Hahn
Lead Pastor, Encounter at Bible Fellowship Church
Ventura, CA

"Mark's story is one based not on theory, but on his real-life story, and aren't those always the best? His story reveals the truth that the longer you hold a grudge, the longer the grudge has hold of you. Mark's story and insights will help you release the grip of the grudge and move forward in freedom."

Jeff Henderson
Lead Pastor, Gwinnett Church (North Point Ministries)
Metro Atlanta, GA

"Mark has started a conversation that the Church has desperately needed to have for a long time. Forgiveness isn't quick and easy when you've been deeply hurt. But it's so necessary. Mark helps us get unstuck when we don't know how to actually move closer to Jesus in the process. Do yourself a favor and read this book."

Ben Reed
Small Groups Pastor, Saddleback Church, Lake Forest Campus
Lake Forest, CA
Author of *Starting Small: The Ultimate Small Group Blueprint*

"Pastor Riggins has written a highly informative book on how to forgive from the Christian perspective. He uses engaging stories and much practical, Bible-based advice to help the hurting learn how to forgive and be free of the resentments which can rob one of joy."

Dr. Robert Enright, Ph.D.
Professor of Educational Psychology
University of Wisconsin-Madison
Co-founder, International Forgiveness Institute
Author of *The Forgiving Life*

STUCK

When You Want to Forgive but
Don't Know How

Mark Riggins *with* Blake Atwood

Stuck: When You Want to Forgive but Don't Know How

Copyright © 2014 by Mark Riggins.

Edited by Blake Atwood with EditFor.me.

Published by Rainer Publishing.
www.rainerpublishing.com

ISBN 978-0692339978

All Scripture quotations, unless otherwise indicated, are taken from The Holy Bible, New International Version ®, NIV ®. Copyright © 1973, 1978, 1984, 2011 by Biblica, Inc. ™

To my Dad: Jim Riggins
You were the fastest forgiver I've ever known.

Looking forward to our reunion day!

Contents

Acknowledgments

As I wrote on Saturday mornings, it was not unusual for my wife Ginger to text me a picture of a Christian bookstore's bookshelf with a message that read, "Can't wait to see your book on this shelf! It's going to help so many people." No matter how many bookshelves hold or don't hold this book, it will always mean more to me that my wife Ginger persistently believes in me.

A team of incredibly insightful people read early drafts and provided critical feedback: Ginger Riggins, Dr. Daniel Hahn, Jack Monroe, Dr. J. Robin Maxson, Ben Wilson, Larry Valenzuela, Scott Tanksley, and Jan Anderson. Thank you all for making this a much better book.

Most of all, thank you Heavenly Father for providing unlimited forgiveness to me.

FOREWORD

Imagine experiencing a loss that makes you richer, an injury that makes you stronger, or a scar that makes you more beautiful. Such is the miraculous power of forgiveness in healing a wound.

But it isn't easy.

Forgiveness is hard because it isn't fair. The victim shouldn't be required to pay twice, we think. But there's an ironic twist to forgiveness. The one who practices it, truly, connects personally with the heart of God at a deeper level than may be possible through any other experience of life. Genuine forgiveness is transformative and ends up being worth far more than its cost.

Mark Riggins found out about this the hard way. When he was wounded by a friend and set out to obey Christ's command to forgive, he didn't know how to do it. And he didn't know anyone who could tell him. So he did his homework—in the Scriptures and the writings of theologians and counselors—and learned life-changing lessons. Then he created this resource, a kind of tutorial on how to forgive, for others who might find themselves in the same predicament.

What Mark learned is that forgiveness is a process one works through in partnership with God. That process is not mechanical, but it does involve essential ingredients. Mark helpfully identifies these "steps" and explains and illustrates them. He also provides practical exercises to guide the reader on their own journey. His insights are organized by means of an acronym: S.A.V.I.O.R. But this is more than a clever outline. It is the key that unlocks the mysteries of forgiveness. Whatever our quandaries—and there are many—the answer is Jesus. Mark shows us how Jesus gives the answer and then explains what to do about it.

This is a short book. But if you read it and do what it says, it could give you your life back.

J. Robin Maxson, D.Min.
Pastor Emeritus, United Evangelical Free Church, Klamath Falls, OR
Author of *"I Do" or Do I?* and *Singleness, Marriage, and the Will of God.*

CHAPTER 1

The Day My Best Friend Fired Me

*"Everyone says forgiveness is a lovely idea
until they have something to forgive."*
— C.S. Lewis

As soon as I read the email from my pastor, my heart skipped a beat: "Mark, come to my office first thing this morning."

You know that feeling when you sense something isn't right? I told my wife about the odd email, then I drove to the church.

As I walked into my mentor's large office, he said, "Hey man, why don't you close the door?" My heart was pounding. I shut the door and sat in the green wingback chair facing his desk. This man whom I'd worked alongside for so long began reading a prepared letter. Apparently, there would be no small talk. I didn't know it, but he was about to make a shocking announcement and instantly end our friendship.

My mind replayed our relationship like a DVR on rewind: when we flew to Boston to watch the Red Sox play the Yankees at Fenway Park, when we flew to Chicago to tour Wrigley Field, the many times we drove to The Ballpark in Arlington to catch a Ranger's game. We'd even watched countless games of baseball and basketball at each other's houses.

He was the senior pastor and I was his associate pastor, his "right-hand man," the Tim Cook to his Steve Jobs (minus the fame, money, and power, but you get the point).

To be blunt, we were a great ministry duo.

During the twelve years we worked together, the church had more than tripled in weekly attendance, financial giving, and staff members. Due to that kind of growth, we relocated to a much larger campus. We also transitioned an established church to use a relevant ministry style. As ministry leaders know, that much time "in the trenches" together forms a unique bond!

The man reading this prepared letter was not just my pastor; he was one of my best friends. We genuinely loved each other.

That's what made his announcement so gut-wrenching.

THE BACKSTORY

Eighteen months earlier, I sat in that same green chair and told my pastor I felt drawn to lead a church with a unique focus on reaching people outside of the church.

Seeking his wisdom, I asked, "Should I pastor an existing church or start a new one?"

He was supportive and encouraged me to start a new church. Now we just needed to decide where.

A year later, I returned to my friend's office with some great news: I'd found a church-planting partner in North Point Community Church, pastored by Andy Stanley. I was thrilled with this prospect because they had proven themselves successful in starting churches focused on the exact kind of people I wanted to reach—those outside of the church. But we still needed to decide where this new church was going to be planted. Little did I know then that this issue would ultimately soil our relationship.

During the next few months, I felt our relationship cooling. I sensed my friend pulling away from me, despite the fact that I desperately wanted his help in discerning God's will for this next phase. We'd always made major decisions together. He said he felt unqualified to help me with this process because he'd never personally started a church.

Several days prior to the day my best friend fired me, I told him that after much research and prayer, the leadership at North Point Ministries and I believed it made sense to plant this new "church for the unchurched" right there in our hometown. I requested that his church and my new church form a partnership, then I asked to transition officially out of my current role in three months. I also offered to stay longer or leave sooner if he preferred.

BACK TO THE DAY MY BEST FRIEND
FIRED ME

As he read from his prewritten letter, he announced that my resignation was effective immediately and there would be no partnership between our churches. He said starting a new church in the same town would hurt the church he pastored, so he didn't believe God would lead me to do such a thing. As he continued reading, I felt the sting and shock of unexpected, unfriendly phrases like, "This Sunday will be your last day," and "Have your office cleaned out by Monday morning."

When he finished, he looked up and calmly asked, "Do you have any questions?"

We sat without speaking, a moment of silence for the death of our friendship. Then I said the only words that seemed appropriate, "I hate that it's ending this way." He agreed. I stood up and slowly walked out of his office. I already felt something hurting deep inside of me. My mind raced in a thousand different directions simultaneously.

Now what was I supposed to do?

Suddenly, I had no income, and I feared our church members would feel the pressure to take sides. Plus, I'd just lost one of my best friends. After serving together for twelve years, our relationship seemed irrevocably severed. We wouldn't talk to each other for years to come. I walked out to the parking lot, each step heavier than the last.

I sat alone, motionless in my car, confusion and bitterness racing circles round my mind.

TWO WEEKS AFTER THE "BREAK-UP"

In the early aftermath of this professional and relational catastrophe, a friend told me, "Take a few days off, Mark. Get away, clear your head, and work on your heart before rushing into the next season of your life."

My wife and I both thought that wise advice, so we loaded up our Suburban and drove to Junction, TX, a familiar family getaway on the Llano River and a much-needed change of scenery at this particular point in my life.

I had one goal that weekend: to be completely healed by Monday morning.

I'm not kidding.

God wanted that. I wanted that. So why not? "Let's do this!" I thought.

I spent the weekend reading Scripture, praying, crying, journaling, walking, playing with my kids, and talking with my wife. I knew God was going to use this experience to shape me. I just needed him to do it by Monday morning!

That weekend I drove the proverbial stake in the ground to heal and move forward. I felt a twinge of hope. Monday morning came and I was determined to go home and be a healthy husband, father, and pastor. I could hear "Eye of the Tiger" from the *Rocky III* soundtrack in my head.

Come hell or high water, I was leaving my hurt in Junction, TX.

So we piled back into our Suburban, turned on some upbeat music, and began the drive home. Now new friends accompanied me: determination and hope. Ninety miles later, as we neared our hometown, something trivial caught my attention.

The "U.S. Highway 87" sign, which led to my former job, triggered an unexpected internal fight. Immediately, I felt a surprising surge of emotional pain from a deep place in my heart.

Hurt brought his old friends anger and fear, and they quickly beat the living daylights out of hope and determination. In their dark and cruel way, they screamed that healing had never really happened. I felt discouraged and confused. "Eye of the Tiger" segued into a bugle playing "Taps" at a funeral. And all because of an otherwise innocent highway sign!

My hurt was turning into a grudge.

For the first time, I felt involuntarily attached to my past.

For the first time, I felt stuck.

FAST-FORWARD TWO YEARS

"Mark, you keep looking back. You need to forgive and start moving forward."

My well-intentioned, church-planting coach and friend from North Point Ministries had heard my two-year-old sob story before. On this day, as we sat across from each other at Smokejack BBQ in Alpharetta, GA, I chided myself for yet again rehashing what should have been ancient history.

I took a deep breath and nodded my head in agreement, like you do when someone says something completely true but completely unhelpful. "Forgive and move forward?" I thought. "Sure. No problem. While I'm at it I'll solve world hunger and negotiate world peace. I want to move forward but I don't know how. That's the problem. I'm stuck!"

Once back at my West Texas home, I dug deeper within, hoping to pray a more genuine prayer of forgiveness. To my horror, my nasty grudge returned a couple days later. Over the next few weeks, I experienced that same vicious cycle: a prayer of forgiveness, followed by a returning grudge, followed by another prayer of forgiveness, followed by a returning grudge.

To be given a memory capable of instant and detailed recall without the ability to forget feels like the cruelest divine trick of all. My grudge was the heaviest weight to carry but the hardest burden to put down.

I was desperate. Well-meaning people advised, "You gotta forgive and move on." Honestly, and this is *not* pastoral advice, I wanted to slap 'em!

"What specifically can I do?" I thought. "Please! Somebody tell me! How do I forgive and move forward?"

I was exhausted.

Something had to change.

WHAT'S YOUR STUCK STORY?

Can you relate? Have you been deeply hurt?

Maybe you've experienced something much more painful than me. Your ex-spouse, a parent, a co-worker, or a close friend may have hurt you.

Someone did something to you.

Someone took something from you.

Someone owes you something.

Your hurt may include a divorce, bankruptcy, a job loss, betrayal, abuse, or broken trust. The day you're hurt is a bad day, but the unrelenting weight of a heavy grudge is even worse, isn't it?

When you want to forgive but don't know how, you feel stuck.

Don't know if you're stuck? Consider these questions:

- Have you told your story more than once to the same person?
- Do you reference your hurt as an event, mentioning the people and the circumstances?
- Do you replay the event at least once a day in your mind?
- Do you have imaginary conversations with the person who hurt you?
- When you think about your pain, does it cause a mental fog?
- Is it hard to explain to others why your hurt bothers you so much?
- Does your story focus primarily on your pain and what you've lost?
- Have you made a commitment to yourself to *not* tell your story again and then have broken that commitment?

If you answered *yes* to any of these questions, chances are you're stuck.

Being stuck is exhausting. It's like plodding through pudding. Your life feels like it's happening in slow motion. Your dreams are on hold. You want to forgive, but you can't.

Be encouraged though: you're not the only one walking in pudding.

In a nationwide Gallup poll, 94 percent of people said it was important to forgive, but 85 percent said they would need outside help in order to forgive. Apparently, many of us are stuck, and just because Christianity focuses on forgiveness doesn't mean we're adept at it. Many of us fail to fully forgive. Why is that?

We don't know how! As John Ortberg says, "Many of us struggle, not so much with understanding the message of forgiveness, but with living in the reality of it."

In my past, I was often not terribly helpful when it came to forgiveness since I tended to focus more on the *why* and *what* of forgiveness instead of the *how*.

If a church member had asked me, "How do I overcome an addiction?" I would have replied, "Here are a few specific steps you can take . . ."

If a church member had asked me, "How do I grow my faith?" I would have replied, "Here are a few specific steps you can take . . ."

If a church member had asked me, "How do I forgive?" I would have replied, "Just do it!"

Aren't you glad I wasn't your pastor?

So where should we go to discover *how* to forgive?

Jesus Christ, "History's Greatest Forgiver," is the most qualified person to teach us how to forgive. He spent his years on earth demonstrating exactly how to forgive. He lived history's only grudge-free life. He's forgiven the most people *ever*. Plus, he forgives me and you, and we both know how much our souls need that on a daily basis.

In this book, I identify six forgiveness behaviors that Jesus modeled. These six steps are not theoretical, but real, practical steps that will help you avoid common roadblocks to deep and lasting forgiveness. True forgiveness doesn't occur by checking six steps off of your to-do list, but rather these steps will position you to allow the Holy Spirit to transform your heart into a heart that fully forgives.

But first, a WARNING: if you don't learn how to forgive, pride and resentment will eventually crush you. You already know people like that. So do I. One day they were hurt, then every following day they got a little bit colder. As years passed, the weight of their grudge deformed them. Now they're only hard, bitter people.

When you're stuck, doing nothing will cost you everything.

Jesus, who gave everything to set you free, wants you to know how to forgive and get unstuck.

GET UNSTUCK: PUTTING IT TO WORK

1. Acknowledge that what you've been doing isn't working. Make a commitment to complete the process of forgiveness no matter what.

2. Write a paragraph describing what life would be like for you if you were able to finally forgive. Use a positive voice rather than a negative voice. For example, instead of writing "I won't roll my eyes every time I hear his name," write "I could experience peace regardless of my circumstances."

3. Tell someone about your decision and ask him or her to pray for you. There is something meaningful about sharing your decision with someone else.

4. Spend time asking God for wisdom, strength, and his presence throughout this process.

Now, let me pray for you:

God, you know the heart of the person sitting in front of these words right now. You know the details of their pain, their discouragement, and their fatigue. Father, would you comfort and encourage them? Forgiveness is close to your heart. Forgiveness is why you sacrificed your most precious gift, your Son. We need your strength to start and complete this process. "Now to him who is able to do immeasurably more than all we ask or imagine, according to his power that is at work within us." Amen.

CHAPTER 2

FOURTEEN THINGS
FORGIVENESS IS NOT

"To err is human, to forgive, divine."
— Alexander Pope

FORGIVENESS IS DIFFICULT, BUT IF YOU MISUNDERSTAND it, it's impossible. Before you begin the six-step process described in the next six chapters, be sure you understand what forgiveness is not.

I misunderstood one little thing about forgiveness, and I became stuck.

A SMALL MISUNDERSTANDING

"I've made a cake!"

My sisters and I were children at the time, but even we could tell how proud our dad was of this rare accomplishment. Mom normally cooked and baked, but for reasons still unknown to this day, Dad baked a cake for us. We were famished kids returning from school, so we didn't much care who had made the cake or for what reason.

It didn't even bother us that the cake was *green*.

It's not that the icing was green. The cake *itself* was green.

And no, it wasn't St. Patrick's Day either.

Still, it was cake, and it was ours.

After dinner Dad cut the odd-colored cake, and we took our first glorious bite. It was incredible . . . until our taste buds kicked in. Confusion reigned when our expectations collided with our experience.

It looked like cake, had the texture of cake, but it tasted more like . . . cornbread. Cornbread? That's right. We were eating green cornbread!

Dad laughed. "Well, the recipe called for flour, but I substituted cornmeal. I tried to cover it up with food coloring and extra sugar. I guess I misunderstood the importance of flour."

Yes Dad. You did.

Now, why would my Dad think even for a minute that cornmeal could replace flour? Did someone tell him that? Did he just assume that? Who knows? It was a rookie mistake. His baking skills were green in every sense of the word.

Yet who am I to judge?

Looking back on my failed attempts at forgiveness, my essential mistake was also based on one early misunderstanding. For some reason, I thought forgiveness could be achieved through a one-time decision followed by a one-time prayer.

Forgiveness doesn't work like sticking a dollar bill into a soda machine and getting a Dr. Pepper in return, but that's how I was approaching it. After inserting my prayer of forgiveness, I expected healing and forgiveness to be immediately dispensed.

That was my misunderstanding. I don't know where I ever heard that or why I believed that. Why did I think forgiveness was a one-time prayer? Did someone tell me that? Did I just make it up? I have no idea! It was a rookie mistake.

My misunderstanding created a vicious cycle. I would pray a genuine prayer of forgiveness, then something would remind me of my past, my hurt would return, and I'd become frustrated that my forgiveness didn't take. So I'd pray another prayer of forgiveness, try to dig deeper, only to have my hurt return a few days later. It was maddening!

To make matters worse, I assumed most people forgave others easily.

What was wrong with my faith? Why was I stuck?

I was stuck because of a basic misunderstanding. I thought forgiveness was a one-time transaction instead of an ongoing process. Do you have a misunderstanding about forgiveness? If so, it may be keeping you stuck. I've put together a list of the top Fourteen "Things Forgiveness is Not" to help you discover if you have a misunderstanding. Read the list and see if any strike a nerve.

FOURTEEN THINGS
FORGIVENESS IS NOT[1]

1. Forgiveness is not neglecting justice.

You can forgive and still call the police. This became personal for Ginger and me when someone burglarized our home. Several weeks later, the police found and arrested our criminals. Though we forgave them, we were ready to prosecute.

The distinction between forgiveness and justice is important. Forgiveness does not require releasing the criminal from the penalty of their crime. Forgiveness releases you from the hurt and grudge of the criminal's crime. As Stormie Omartian says, "Forgiveness doesn't make the other person right; it makes you free."

2. Forgiveness is not reconciliation.

It takes one person to forgive and two people to reconcile. Reconciliation is ideal but rarely reality. In many cases, reconciliation is a bad idea. It would be wise to forgive an abusive ex-spouse but unwise to reconcile with him or her.

Forgiveness is between you and God. Your offender doesn't have a role in your decision. Forgiveness doesn't require you to reconnect or even notify your offender of your decision. Your offender's opinion on your forgiveness is irrelevant. Forgiveness is a solo sport; reconciliation is a team sport. We'll discuss more about reconciliation in Chapter 11.

3. Forgiveness is not corporate.

You forgive individual people, but not companies or churches. It's tempting to forgive companies where you experience hurt because it feels less messy than identifying specific individuals. However, corporations and organizations don't hurt people. People hurt people.

There may be a group of people whose actions (or inaction) have hurt you. You can't forgive a group, but you can forgive individuals that comprise the group. To start the process, it may help to identify the person who hurt you most. Then work through the process forgiving each person individually in the company or church.

4. Forgiveness is not broad.

You forgive specific hurts, not general behavior. If you break your left arm, you don't wear a full-body cast. In the same way, real forgiveness addresses a specific injury. Andy Stanley has said, "General forgiveness does not heal specific hurts. It's important to pinpoint what was taken from you." Chapter 4 will walk you through an important assessment on this matter.

5. Forgiveness is not fast.

Deep hurts need more time and often need a second coat. The deeper the hurt, the longer forgiveness takes. Fast forgiveness fades. Forgiveness is a cycle that often needs to be repeated.

After breaking my arm as a kid, the doctor put it in a cast. Several weeks later he cut off the cast, but an X-ray revealed that the bone wasn't completely healed. He put another, smaller cast back on for a few more weeks. Eventually, my broken bone healed.

Forgiveness is a similar process. You may take every "proper step," but forgiveness still takes time. It may require you to walk through the six steps in this book more than once in order to heal completely. Be patient with yourself. This may be the most difficult, *and the most rewarding*, experience of your life.

6. Forgiveness is not forgetting.

You may remember what they did, but now you'll also remember that you forgave.

Lewis Smedes writes, "A healed memory is not a deleted memory."

Why did God design you that way? Wouldn't it be easier if you could forget it? Maybe. But perhaps God wants your painful memory to be a reminder that you are constantly dependent upon his grace. Remembering healed pain you overcame because of his grace can become a positive memory.

Either way, your painful memory will now be accompanied by your brave choice to forgive. You can reshape something dark and ugly into something mysteriously beautiful. We'll address this further in Chapter 9.

7. Forgiveness does not diminish their actions.

Forgiveness recognizes that sin (yours and your offender's) sent Christ to the cross. There's a distinction between overlooking and forgiving. Forgiveness takes an honest look at injustice. Forgiveness does not whitewash.

Forgiveness is strong enough to overcome someone's ugliest behavior. God didn't diminish or overlook the ugliness of our sin. He forgave by sending his Son to the cross. Forgiveness is brutally honest.

8. Forgiveness is not weakness.

Confronting your deepest pain and choosing to forgive is not for the faint-hearted. Avoiding forgiveness is a sign of weakness. Forgiveness requires a personal confrontation with your deepest pain. When you begin the forgiveness process, you've begun to lift heavy weights at the spiritual gym. Gandhi spoke to this when he said, "The weak can never forgive. Forgiveness is the attribute of the strong."

9. Forgiveness is not trusting.

Forgiveness is a gift you offer while trust is something your offender earns. If your neighbors rob your home, you can forgive them without giving them a key to your home. If every time your friend calls and they say something hurtful, you can forgive him or her without answering their calls. Forgiveness is a gift you offer. Trust is something they earn.

10. Forgiveness is not enabling.

You can forgive and still confront. You can forgive an abusive spouse without allowing that person to continue their behavior. In fact, forgiveness may require you to confront the offender if they're hurting themselves. In John

8:11, Jesus told the woman caught in adultery, "Go now and leave your life of sin." Always forgive, but never enable.

11. Forgiveness is not tolerating.

You can forgive past behavior without subjecting yourself to their present behavior. Your forgiveness benefits you and honors God. However, the other person's behavior may never change. That's between them and God.

If a friend is hurting you, forgive and walk away. In Matthew 18:15-17, Jesus says that it is appropriate for you to forgive them but no longer tolerate their behavior.

12. Forgiveness is not waiting for an apology.

Forgiveness is your choice. An apology is your offender's choice. Your forgiveness has *nothing* to do with your offender. Some people are unaware that they've hurt you, and some people don't care that they've hurt you.

Waiting for an apology puts your offender in charge of your forgiveness and ultimately your spiritual growth. Do you want them to have that kind of power or influence over you?

But what if they don't deserve it?

Grace that's earned isn't grace.

Christian forgiveness is always for those who don't deserve it.

13. Forgiveness is not dismissing emotions or avoiding pain.

Forgiveness allows your anger and pain to push you toward grace. Your pain and emotions are real. Instead of running from them, identify them. Just like a budget clarifies what's going on with your finances, an honest look at your emotions clarifies what's going on in your heart. Chapter 10 will walk you through that process.

14. Forgiveness is not a single prayer.

Forgiveness is a process (seventy times seven) resembling a marathon, not a sprint. Prayer is a vital part of forgiveness. But most of us will need more than one prayer. My wife runs half-marathons and has never invited me to run with her on the morning of a race. Why? Preparing for something that significant requires a training process, and I don't run. Forgiving a deep hurt may be the hardest thing God ever asks you to do, so don't expect it to happen instantly.

The next six chapters include six steps, or behaviors, that Jesus practiced while on earth. To help you remember these six steps, let's use the word S.A.V.I.O.R., as each letter represents one of the six behaviors:

- Stop telling your story as a victim.
- Assess your hurt.
- Value your offender.
- Intercede for your offender.
- Own your part.
- Release their debt.
- When I followed these six steps, I finally forgave.
- I pray you will too.

GET UNSTUCK: PUTTING IT TO WORK

1. Identify one or more forgiveness misunderstandings you have believed to be true.
2. How has this misunderstanding prevented forgiveness?

CHAPTER 3

STOP TELLING YOUR STORY
AS A VICTIM

*"The best time for you to hold your tongue
is the time you feel you must say something or bust."*
— Josh Billings

❝I NEED A TIME OUT.”

With those five simple words, Lori's life changed. She didn't know how drastic the change would be, but she knew this wasn't an off-the-cuff remark from her husband Mike. She heard those words while the two of them were taking a familiar drive from their church in Santa Barbara to their home in Carpinteria. The scenery was beautiful and peaceful, a stark contrast to the plummeting, surreal feeling churning around in Lori's gut.

"A time out? What are you talking about?" Lori was confused and frustrated, and her clipped tone conveyed as much. Matter-of-factly, Mike answered, "I need some space. I'm tired of taking care of everyone else. I'm going to start taking care of me now, so I'm going to move out of the house for awhile and find an apartment to live in."

Up until Mike's surprising announcement, Lori had been naively peaceful, like a deer eating corn unaware it's being watched through a hunter's scope, but Mike's piercing words shattered her world like an unannounced bullet. He was pulling the trigger on their twenty-three-year marriage.

It soon became clear that he'd been planning his exit for a long time. A few days later on the pool deck in their backyard, Mike gathered their four children, ages seventeen, eighteen, twenty, and twenty-two, and informed them that he was going to "take a break and live in another house for awhile."

Despite her frustration, Lori knew Mike's decision was out of her control. After twenty-three years of marriage, Mike divorced Lori.

Suddenly, he was just gone.

FAST-FORWARD SEVERAL YEARS

As I sat on a couch across from Lori, she agreed to revisit that painful time. I hesitantly asked, "What was your life like immediately after Mike left?"

"Well, it was terrible," she began. "I was consumed with self-pity. I felt like an old shoe thrown on the floor. I felt rejected and betrayed. I didn't know what to do. Our public identities were completely tied together. Up until then, Mike was a respected businessman in our community and leader in our church. I had a highly visible job within the school district and was active in our church. After Mike left, I was hurt, mad, and scared."

Lori told me how her world fell apart around her, and she stopped taking care of herself, losing weight and becoming unusually thin. "I became so thin that I looked as if I was fighting for my life. People began noticing my unusual appearance. Those who hadn't heard the news would ask me, 'Is everything okay Lori?' At first, I loved that question. I would quickly paint Mike with the blackest paintbrush. I'd tell them, 'My husband left me. My life is turned upside down. And now I'm having health problems.' If they would allow me to continue my story, I would tell them that he probably left me for a younger woman. Then I would pass along any mean things that came to mind."

Lori was honest with me and with herself about how she relished telling people her story. "Initially, it stirred up sympathy and people would rally around to support me. But after awhile, I noticed something changed. Eventually, people seemed less enthusiastic to hear my story. Some people were even resistant when I would tell it."

As I listened, I was fascinated to see this side of Lori. Those who know her would describe her as an extremely positive person and a genuine bright light that's always shining.

So I asked her how in the world she had transitioned from the helpless victim she was describing into the generous person sitting across from me.

That's when Lori said something keen that gave me insight into how *not* to hold a grudge: "My closest friend challenged me. When she'd hear me begin to tell my victim story, she'd say, 'All right, it's time to change the song.' She was right."

THE NEVERENDING (VICTIM) STORY

Can you relate to Lori?

Do you tell your victim story to whoever will listen? If so, how often?

Two things tend to happen following a deep hurt, and we rarely connect the dots between the two:

1. We tell our victim story.
2. We struggle to forgive.

Turns out our story *is* part of the problem. Victim stories can bring comfort, but they sabotage us. Every time we tell someone what our offender did to us, we strike a match in our heart to light the bitter flame once again. Telling your victim story might be fun initially, but it will ultimately serve to only keep you stuck.

The Apostle Paul warns us about this. Before telling us to "Be kind and compassionate to one another, forgiving each other, just as in Christ, God forgave you," Paul tells us in Ephesians 4:31-32 to "Get rid of all bitterness, rage and anger, brawling and slander, along with every form of malice."

Lori eventually realized that even though her story was satisfying to tell, it was keeping her stuck. The more she told her story, the more she saw herself as a victim and the more it triggered negative emotions.

Ever been there? Maybe you're there now.

I know this about you because I know it about me—you're telling a story. For every painful event, you create a story. Even if you're not telling anyone else your story, you're telling yourself your story. So, what's your story? Can you recall it right now? I see three important reasons to understand the story you're telling yourself and others.

Reason #1: Your Story Triggers Memories with Similar Emotions

Your mind is a filing cabinet full of categorized memories. Every time you recall a memory from the anger category, you can't help but to access the other anger memories filed nearby. When you recall a memory from the victim category, you access nearby victim memories.

When Lori told her story about how Mike had hurt her, she'd remember other examples of how she had been hurt, especially by Mike. Misery loves company, and so do miserable memories. Your victim story triggers other painful memories.

Reason #2: Your Story Isolates You

Every time you tell your story as a victim, you further isolate yourself from friends and family. An offense can hurt you, but repeating your story as a victim removes your warmth. You will unintentionally push people away by rehashing your self-focused victim story. You want to draw sympathy and support, but your story sounds like a broken record to those closest to you, and people can endure that kind of noise for only so long.

Lori noticed people's initial sympathy transition into resistance as she continued telling her story. A wise friend loved her enough to say, "It's time to change your song." If you're telling a victim story, let me be a friend by saying, "It's time to change your song." Otherwise, your victim story will isolate you.

Reason #3: Your Story Reveals Your Heart

Like an MRI reveals the internal details of your body, your story reveals the internal condition of your heart. As Luke 6:45 says, "For the mouth speaks what the heart is full of." The public words coming out of your mouth announce the precise condition of your private heart.

Lori's story revealed that she was still hurting, that she saw herself as a victim, and that she blamed her present situation on her past hurt. Lori's words confirmed her heart was hurting, bitter, and bent on blaming others.

Your story is your heart's MRI as it reveals what's really going on in your heart. Therefore, it's critical to monitor what you're saying to others and what you allow your mind to dwell on.

JESUS' VICTIM STORY

Did Jesus ever tell his story as a victim? He surely experienced hurt and betrayal. Remember, he was:

- Betrayed by his friend Judas
- Abandoned by his closest friends, the disciples
- Rejected by the religious at Caiaphas' Council
- Physically and emotionally assaulted by strangers

- Humiliated in public by Herod
- Falsely condemned by Pilate
- Publicly crucified

If anyone was ever entitled to tell his story as a victim, it was Jesus. But he didn't. Instead, Scripture points out that Jesus often did something odd.

He was despised and rejected by mankind, a man of suffering, and familiar with pain. Like one from whom people hide their faces he was despised, and we held him in low esteem. Surely he took up our pain and bore our suffering, yet we considered him punished by God, stricken by him, and afflicted. But he was pierced for our transgressions, he was crushed for our iniquities; the punishment that brought us peace was on him, and by his wounds we are healed. We all, like sheep, have gone astray, each of us has turned to our own way; and the Lord has laid on him the iniquity of us all. He was oppressed and afflicted, yet **he did not open his mouth**; he was led like a lamb to the slaughter, and as a sheep before its shearers is **silent**, so **he did not open his mouth**. — Isaiah 53:3-7, emphasis added

"When he was accused by the chief priests and the elders, **he gave no answer**. Then Pilate asked him, 'Don't you hear the testimony they are bringing against you?' But **Jesus made no reply**, not even to a single charge—to the great amazement of the governor." — Matthew 27:12-14, emphasis added

Jesus said nothing.

No story.

Silence.

If his answers had been transcribed, it would have read "...."

As I read the verses, I feel myself begging Jesus to defend himself and shout something like, "People, I'm innocent! I'm holy. I'm your creator. I could speak and the earth would swallow you up. I could dropkick you from Jerusalem to Rome! Don't you know who I am?"

That's what I want him to say.

That's the story I would shout.

This treatment of Jesus isn't fair! These people obviously misunderstood Jesus and his motives.

Why didn't Jesus speak up to clear things up?

He could have at least said something like, "People, I'm here to save you. After all, I created you and I know you intimately. I left Heaven so that we can have a relationship and spend eternity together. I love you that much. I'm here to forgive you completely."

But our Savior said *nothing*.

The maker of vocal cords waited in complete silence.

I envision extended periods of awkward, pin-drop silence in Pilate's court. Even today, we're struck dumb by Jesus' non-answer answers. Why didn't he speak?

Because Jesus knew something we forget: words get in the way.

Jesus taught that forgiveness isn't found in speaking, but in surrendering.

He taught that forgiveness isn't found in argument, but in action.

He taught that forgiveness isn't found in defending, but in dying.

YOUR VICTIM STORY

Lori's story was getting in the way. Maybe yours has too. Step one in the forgiveness process is to—you guessed it—stop telling your story as a victim. Are you ready to lay down your story?

Now, that doesn't mean you should carry your burden alone. It's important to choose one or two people, like your spouse, a close friend, a pastor, or a counselor with whom you can share your story.

But stop telling everyone else.

Period.

Remain silent.

Even pin-drop, awkwardly silent.

If anyone specifically asks about your hurt—other than the one or two people you've chosen as trusted listeners—say something like, "Thanks for asking. I'd rather not talk about it, but know that I'm working to forgive, and I'd appreciate your prayers." In Chapter 9, we'll discuss how to write a new story to replace the one you've been telling yourself and others. But first, follow the behavior of our SAVIOR and stop telling your story as a victim.

GET UNSTUCK: PUTTING IT TO WORK

1. Write your story in one paragraph that best represents how you're currently telling it—not how you wish you were telling it, but how you're actually currently telling it.

2. Keeping it to one paragraph may be hard, but the effort to summarize will be worth it. Writing out your story creates a starting point from which you can move forward. Since your story reveals the condition of your heart, as your heart heals, you will look back on this story and see progress.

3. Let one or two trusted people know that you're choosing to stop telling your victim story and allow them to help you keep that commitment. In Chapter 9, we'll talk about how to write a new story. In the meantime, stop telling your story as a victim. It will always block forgiveness.

4. Memorize Isaiah 53:7: "He was oppressed and afflicted, yet he did not open his mouth; he was led like a lamb to the slaughter, and as a sheep before its shearers is silent, so he did not open his mouth."

CHAPTER 4

Assess Your Hurt

"General forgiveness does not heal specific hurts.
It's important to pinpoint what was taken from you."
— Andy Stanley

"WHERE'S KEVIN? I SAID, WHERE'S KEVIN?"

Jason, twenty-six, had barged into Kevin's home. Little did fourteen-year-old Kevin know then that his life was about to dramatically change.

In that moment while tying his shoes, Kevin's mind was focused on the basketball practice he was about to attend. He wasn't prepared for such an interruption, and he surely wasn't prepared for what was about to happen.

Kevin had asked his friend to answer the door, then felt immediate fear as he heard Jason's loud questions. In an instant, Kevin recalled an otherwise innocent moment from a few weeks earlier, when his dad was throwing a baseball with him out on the street in front of their house. A wayward throw had struck Jason's prized truck. Apparently, such an infraction was enough cause to send Jason into a rage.

When Kevin approached the door, he noticed a pistol in Jason's hand. Jason then lifted the gun, pointed it at Kevin, and pulled the trigger. CRACK! The shot sounded like Jason's truck backfiring. The bullet narrowly missed Kevin and pierced the couch. Instantly filled with terror, Kevin ran toward the dining room.

Those would be his final steps.

Kevin heard another backfire—CRACK!—and felt a sting in the back of his neck. He immediately fell to floor.

In that moment, Kevin's life changed forever. Though he lived, he would now live as a quadriplegic. In an instant, an active teenage boy full of dreams became a teenage boy dependent on others for basic necessities like bathing, going to the bathroom, getting dressed, and transportation.

FAST-FORWARD TWENTY YEARS

I'm sitting in a coffee shop with Kevin as he sits in his wheelchair. He enjoys drinking mocha frappuccinos, but holding the cup sometimes proves to be a challenge. He spins the cup while snapping at it with his finger and thumb until he feels confident enough in his grip to pick it up for a drink.

Eventually I ask, "Have you forgiven Jason for what he did to you?"

"Yes. But it took awhile."

"You aren't mad at him? How did you forgive someone who did something so terrible?"

"I spent ten years being angry with Jason for shooting me and questioning God for allowing Jason to shoot me. I even turned to alcohol and drugs to try and cope with it all. But after awhile, I became so tired of mentally fighting it all. I was exhausted. I finally decided to surrender and forgive. One of the first things I did was grab a piece of paper and write down all the things I needed to forgive in detail. Being shot created a lot of consequences in my life and my family's life. I wrote it all down so I could fully forgive everything."

ASSESSING YOUR HURT

As you prepare to forgive, take the time to complete this chapter's personal assessment. The goal is to help you identify:

The Injustice: What was done to you?

The Damage: How were you affected?

The Consequences: What has changed as a result?

Injustice: What was done to me?

Begin by asking yourself, "What was done to me?" It might help to look over this list of typical injustices:[2]

- *Emotional absence*: A close person is your life is present physically but feels far away and expresses little love.
- *Physical absence*: A close person in your life is away from you for long periods.
- *Displaced anger*: A close person in your life is angry at someone else but takes it out on you.

- *Excessive anger*: A close person in your life shows intense anger at you without explaining why.
- *Passive anger*: Subtle anger that embarrasses you around others.
- *Ridicule*: A close person in your life makes you feel small and judged.
- *Emotional abuse*: Extreme and persistent anger that damages you psychologically.
- *Physical abuse*: Physical contact that hurts and damages you.
- *Sexual abuse*: Inappropriate touching or physical contact.
- *Excessive anxiety*: Extreme worry that is displaced on you.
- *Excessive punishment*: Deserved punishment that goes way too far.
- *Excessive teasing*: Joking that becomes bullying.
- *Excessive demands*: Consistently asking more than what is reasonable.
- *Harsh judgments*: Expressions that leave you feeling condemned.
- *Ignoring*: A consistent lack of communication that keeps you in the dark.
- *Lack of love*: When someone close to you fails to express any love.
- *Lack of understanding*: When someone close to you does not attempt to understand your viewpoint.
- *Lack of cooperation*: When someone close to you only takes and never gives.

- *Poor decision making*: When someone close to you consistently makes bad choices that affect you.

Do you see your specific injustice on the list? You may have more than one. If you're not sure, ask someone to help you identify them. Take the time to nail it down. The more specific you are, the more helpful it will be.

You'll experience three benefits when you identify your injustice:

Benefit #1: Your identified hurt is less emotionally powerful than your unidentified hurt.

Benefit #2: Your pain becomes normalized when you discover that, though your circumstances are unique, your injustice and pain are not.

Benefit #3: You can now forgive specifically.

Damage: How was I affected?

The second question is: How was I affected?

Kevin's answer to this question was, "I would never walk again."

Think back to Lori's story in the previous chapter. How was Lori affected? She had a broken marriage, obliterated self-worth, and a decreased standard of living (her household income had dropped from two incomes to one).

How were you affected? Here are three questions to help you discover how you were affected:

What was taken?

Kevin lost his ability to walk and lost some of his independence. Lori lost her marriage, her life partner, and her standard of living. As a result of the injustices, what was taken from you?

What was broken?

Kevin lost his identity and became angry with God. After Mike left her, Lori's self-esteem was broken and she saw herself as a helpless victim. As a result of the injustice, what was broken in your life?

What was ruined?

A bullet ruined Kevin's dream of a physically active life. Mike's decision to leave Lori ruined her dream of growing old with her children's dad. As a result of the injustice, what was ruined in your life?

Answering these three questions will help you identify the damage you've experienced. And remember, resist the urge to exaggerate or deny.

Consequences: What has changed as a result?

Ask yourself:

How have I acted since the wound?

How do I feel?

How have I changed?

How have I acted since the wound?

Your own reaction to your injustice may be creating additional painful consequences. Kevin spent several years trying to medicate his pain and became addicted to alcohol and drugs. Lori missed the first four birthday parties of her grandson because she knew Mike would be there and she didn't want to face him. She also experienced a more complicated relationship with her four children.

How have you acted since the wound?

How do I feel?

What emotions does your injustice trigger? Identify your emotions from this list of eight:

8 PRIMARY FEELINGS[3] BY CHIP DODD (CHIPDODD.COM)

Feeling	Benefit
HURT	Names the wound & begins healing
SADNESS	Allows us to value/honor what's present & missed
LONELINESS	Allows us to ask for help, reach out relationally
FEAR	Helps us practice/prepare for accomplishment
ANGER	Helps us tell the truth and dare to hope
SHAME	Awakens us to humility
GUILT	Provides freedom to seek forgiveness
GLADNESS	Reveals the richness of life

Kevin felt anger for several years. Lori felt shame for several years. You have feelings that are a consequence of your injustice. Ask yourself, "When I think about (name your injustice), what's the main emotion I feel?" You may identify more than one.

How have I changed?

Sometimes these wounds build up and, without knowing it, we slip into a pessimistic view of the world.

For years Kevin struggled with questions like:

"What's my purpose?"

"How could God allow this to happen?"

"Why me?"

He was making a bed of cynicism, which felt more and more comfortable the longer he rested there. It's important to self-assess, but consider asking yourself these questions:

"Have I become more cynical or pessimistic since the injustice?"

"Do I like other people more or less since the injustice?"

"Do I like God more or less since the injustice?"

Did Jesus worry about doing an assessment when He forgave? When forgiving the woman at the well, Jesus did not forgive in general. Instead, he identified her specific sins. He could have said, "You're a sinner in need of forgiveness. I forgive all of your sins." Instead, he was specific, mentioning her five previous husbands and the fact that she was living with another man who was not her husband.

Jesus didn't stop there: "Many of the Samaritans from that town believed in him because of the woman's testimony, '**He told me everything I ever did**.' So when the Samaritans came to him, they urged him to stay with them, and he stayed two days. And because of his words many more became believers. They said to the woman, 'We no longer believe just because of what you said; now we have heard for ourselves, and we know that this man really is the Savior of the world." — John 4:39-41

Remember Jesus' parable of the unforgiving servant in Matthew 18? The forgiving king specifically identified how much his servant owed him: exactly 10,000 bags of gold. He didn't forgive in general, but forgave specifically.

General forgiveness is an attempt to avoid pain by taking a forgiveness shortcut. But that road is a dead-end. Make a list by completing this personalized assessment. Identify your injustices, your damage, and your consequences.

GET UNSTUCK: PUTTING IT TO WORK

1. Create a detailed list answering all of the questions below. This personalized assessment will help you identify all that you need to forgive.

   - INJUSTICE: What was done to me?

     Review the list of typical injustices. Identify your injustices.

   - DAMAGE: How was I affected?

     What was taken from me?

     What was broken in my life?

     What was ruined in my life?

     Am I denying or exaggerating the damage I experienced?

   - CONSEQUENCES: What has changed as a result?

     How have I acted since the injustice?

     How do I feel? Ask yourself, "When I think about (name your injustice), what's the main emotion I feel?" Identify your emotions from the list.

     How have I changed? Am I more pessimistic since the injustice?

2. Visit www.mindgarden.com/forgiveness for more detailed measurement tools that can help you discover who and what you need to forgive.

3. Journal your prayers and your experiences as you begin this process. This will record your growth.

4. Here is a simple prayer for you to consider: "Heavenly Father, as you know, forgiveness is difficult

for me. It is a process. Encourage me to take one step forward today. Use this process to shape me to become more like you."

CHAPTER 5

VALUE YOUR OFFENDER

*"We are all full of weakness and errors;
let us mutually pardon each other our follies."*
—Voltaire

PHIL LOST BOTH OF HIS PARENTS INSTANTANEOUSLY—
one to death and one to bitterness.

Phil's dad had been in a terrible accident, and he was prescribed narcotics to relieve his pain. Phil then watched his mom's health decline, and she eventually battled depression. Intending to help, Phil's dad gave some of his prescribed narcotics to Phil's mom. She soon became addicted. Tragically, the narcotics caused a fatal reaction and Phil's mom died at home due to internal bleeding at the age of fifty-nine.

Phil was furious and angry with his father. He blamed his father for his mother's death, for giving her drugs, for not providing adequate care, for living in a rural area where medical emergency response was limited, and for cheating him of the opportunity to introduce his second child to his mom.

Phil's bitterness toward his father grew, and he chose not to have anything to do with him. As if discovering the truth about Santa Claus, Phil became certain that the good father in his memories hadn't ever really existed.

Essentially, Phil had knocked the humanity out of his dad. He had created a *Reality Distortion Field*, a phrase you may know from Star Trek or Steve Jobs. After his mom's death, Phil distorted reality by redefining his dad as nothing more or less than the person who'd contributed to his mom's premature death.

The more innocent Phil made his mom, the guiltier he made his dad. He saw his mom's offenses as understandable, minor offenses. But he saw his dad's offenses as significant, permanent character flaws.

Why did Phil create such a judgmental *Reality Distortion Field*?

Because it justified his bitterness, helped him feel innocent, and allowed him to be less angry with his mom.

As a result, Phil unexpectedly lost both of his parents, and he described those three years as "a numbing haze."

THE HUMAN BEHIND YOUR HURT

How about you? Is your offender nothing more than the person who hurt you? Have you shrunk them down to the size of your hurt?

You may wonder, "Why in the world would I want to value my offender? Can't forgiving them be an act between God and me? Why value my offender?"

The simple answer is: God values them.

He made everyone in his image and sent his Son to redeem them, which leads me to believe that he greatly esteems *all* people.

Plus, God wants to shape you through this step, as difficult as it may seem at first. In Ephesians 4:32, Paul teaches us to value our offender before we forgive them: "Be kind and compassionate to one another, forgiving each other, just as in Christ God forgave you."

Valuing your offender does not remove their guilt.

Read that line again because it's essential to this step in forgiveness. It doesn't mean we condone what they did, but that we believe God's grace is bigger than their sin.

Valuing your offender feels impossible. It *is* hard. But as you struggle through it and embrace God's grace, you *will* mature. Wrestling with grace produces the beauty of forgiveness.

Look to Jesus Christ as your example. He struggled and suffered while forgiving *on the cross*. And how did Jesus value his offenders?

Hanging from the cross, Jesus could still hear echoes of their insults and feel the pulsing of his fresh wounds. They'd cleared their throats on him, pushed him, slapped him, punched him, whipped him, pierced him, mocked him, and were planning to "finish him off."

Then Jesus finally speaks incredible words that have reverberated throughout time, "Father, forgive them . . . "

With saliva mixed with blood still running down his face, Jesus is *already* forgiving them. Imagine the scene as if you'd never heard this story before and consider how absolutely revolutionary Jesus' response is to his tormentors and accusers.

Why? Why is Jesus already forgiving?

Jesus continues, " . . . for they do not know what they are doing."

Jesus saw something I often overlook. I see those who crucified Jesus as sub-human. I don't care about them or their personal hurts, circumstances, ignorance, or fallen conditions. They're nothing but barbaric offenders in my mind.

But Jesus saw something else entirely. Jesus saw them as more than their offenses. Jesus saw people created in his Father's image. He saw broken people in need of forgiveness. He saw people capable of both good and bad.

In 1 Corinthians 2:8, Paul gives us a peek into the inner world of those who crucified Jesus: "None of the rulers of this age understood it, for if they had, they would not have crucified the Lord of glory."

Paul says the people who crucified Jesus had a limited understanding. In his incomparable example while on the cross, Jesus shows us that we should extend grace to those who offend us because they have a limited understanding.

From Heaven, Jesus looks at your offenders and says, "Forgive them. They don't know what they're doing."

FORGIVING REAL PEOPLE

Phil decided three years was long enough. He began the forgiveness process by choosing to see his father as more than just the man who contributed to his mom's death. Phil recognized that, just like himself, his dad was a real person capable of both good and evil.

Phil relied heavily on his faith. Ironically, Phil recognized that his dad was the one who'd introduced him to Christ when he was a little boy. Over time, Phil began to see value in his dad again. Phil destroyed his *Reality Distortion Field* and restored his dad's humanity. Eventually, Phil was able to forgive his dad. Though he hadn't physically lost his dad like he had his mom, Phil's relationship with his dad experienced a resurrection.

Today, Phil and his dad have a good relationship. Phil's family enjoys visits with his dad and his dad's new wife, and Phil is grateful that his dad enjoys a great relationship with his grandchildren. And it all began when Phil learned to value his dad once again.

BEYOND GOOD AND EVIL

When you forget that we're all sinners, it's easy to categorize people as either heroes or villains. But when you remember that we're all broken, it's difficult to categorize people into either a good or evil category.

Andy Stanley says, "In the shadow of my hurt, forgiveness feels like a decision to reward my enemy. But in the shadow of the cross, forgiveness is merely a gift from one undeserving soul to another."

Valuing an offender doesn't turn them into a close friend, a promising parent, or a dependable spouse. You do not condone what they did, but you recognize that they are *more* than what they did. When we remove value from the person who hurt us, we trick ourselves into walking toward a dead-end of bitterness. The process of valuing your offender magnifies God's grace over their sin, and it matures you.

The following short story from theologian Lewis Smedes speaks to our need to humanize those who've hurt us:

THE MAGIC EYES[4] BY LEWIS SMEDES

In the village of Faken in innermost Friesland there lived a long thin baker named Fouke, a righteous man, with a long thin chin and long thin nose. Fouke was so upright that he seemed to spray righteousness from his thin lips over everyone who came near him; so the people of Faken preferred to stay away.

Fouk's wife, Hilda, was short and round, her arms were round, her bosom was round, her rump was round. Hilda did not keep people at bay with righteousness; her soft roundness seemed to invite them instead to come close to her in order to share the warm cheer of her open heart.

Hilda respected her righteous husband, and loved him too, as much as he allowed her; but her heart ached for something more from him than his worthy righteousness.

And there, in the bed of her need, lay the seed of sadness.

One morning, having worked from dawn to knead his dough for the ovens, Fouke came home and found a stranger in his bedroom lying on Hilda's round bosom.

Hilda's adultery soon became the talk of the tavern and the scandal of the Faken congregation. Everyone assumed that Fouke would cast Hilda out of his house, so righteous was he. But he surprised everyone by keeping Hilda as his wife, saying he forgave her as the Good Book said he should.

In his heart of hearts, however, Fouke could not forgive Hilda for bringing shame to his name. Whenever he thought about her, his feelings toward her were angry and hard; he despised her as if she were a common whore. When it came right down to it, he hated her for betraying him after he had been so good and so faithful a husband to her.

He only pretended to forgive Hilda so that he could punish her with his righteous mercy.

But Fouke's fakery did not sit well in heaven.

So each time that Fouke would feel his secret hate toward Hilda, an angel came to him and dropped a small pebble, hardly the size of a shirt button, into Fouke's heart. Each time a pebble dropped, Fouke would feel a stab of pain like the pain he felt the moment he came on Hilda feeding her hungry heart from a stranger's larder.

Thus he hated her the more; his hate brought him pain and his pain made him hate.

The pebbles multiplied. And Fouke's heart grew very heavy with the weight of them, so heavy that the top half of his body bent forward so far that he had to strain his neck upward in order to see straight ahead. Weary with hurt, Fouke began to wish he were dead.

The angel who dropped the pebbles into his heart came to Fouke one night and told him how he could be healed of his hurt.

There was one remedy, he said, only one, for the hurt of a wounded heart. Fouke would need the miracle of the magic eyes. He would need eyes that could look back to the beginning of his hurt and see his Hilda, not as a wife who betrayed him, but as a weak woman who needed him. Only a new way of looking at things through the magic eyes could heal the hurt flowing from the wounds of yesterday.

Fouke protested. "Nothing can change the past," he said. "Hilda is guilty, a fact that not even an angel can change."

"Yes, poor hurting man, you are right," the angel said. "You cannot change the past, you can only heal the hurt that comes to you from the past. And you can heal it only with the vision of the magic eyes."

"And how can I get your magic eyes?" pouted Fouke.

"Only ask, desiring as you ask, and they will be given you. And each time you see Hilda through your new eyes, one pebble will be lifted from your aching heart."

Fouke could not ask at once, for he had grown to love his hatred. But the pain of his heart finally drove him to want and to ask for the magic eyes that the angel had promised. So he asked. And the angel gave.

Soon Hilda began to change in front of Fouke's eyes, wonderfully and mysteriously. He began to see her as a needy woman who loved him instead of a wicked woman who betrayed him.

The angel kept his promise; he lifted the pebbles from Fouke's heart, one by one, though it took a long time to take them all away. Fouke gradually felt his heart grow light; he began to walk straight again, and somehow his nose and his chin seemed less thin and sharp than before. He invited Hilda to come into his heart again, and she came, and together they began again a journey into their second season of humble joy.

Do you see your offender as nothing more than the person who hurt you? Do you need "magic eyes?" Consider the following questions.

GET UNSTUCK: PUTTING IT TO WORK

1. What does it mean to you to know that God loves you despite what you've done?

2. Make a list of things for which you have been forgiven.

3. What was life like for the person (your offender) when he or she was growing up?

4. Do you know of any pain he or she has endured in their lifetime?

5. What was life like for the person at the time of the offense?

6. Can you see this person as a real, broken person full of good and bad?

7. Can you see this person as someone God created in his image?

8. Can you see this person as someone Christ died to forgive?

9. Can you see this offense as something Christ is willing to forgive?

10. Can you see this person as someone God loves despite what they have done?

11. As you begin the process of valuing your offender, it might help to repeat this statement daily for the next week: "Like me, (name) has been wounded. Just as Jesus values me, I value (name). I do not condone or excuse what (name) has done. However, he or she is more than what he or she did to me."

12. Don't forget this encouragement from Scripture: "... for the Lord comforts his people and will have compassion on his afflicted ones." — Isaiah 49:13

CHAPTER 6

Intercede for Your Offender

"The more I pray for an idiot, the less idiotic they become."
— Pastor Daniel Hahn

AFTER MANY YEARS AS A SUCCESSFUL LAWYER, LANCE decided to give back to the community where he grew up by serving as the County Treasurer. For Lance, this would be the "cherry on top" of a fulfilling career.

The community voted him into office and by all appearances the first three years were a huge success. Work was done efficiently, employee morale was high, and public support for Lance was strong.

Lance had no idea that a routine afternoon appointment with one of his staff members was going to turn his world upside down. As Lance listened, the staffer revealed that another member of his staff had stolen several thousand dollars over the past several months. The hair stood up on the back of Lance's neck while his head spun.

"Is this really happening?" he thought.

As soon as the employee left his office, Lance called the sheriff. The sheriff's office conducted an investigation and quickly turned it over to the District Attorney's Office. Their investigation revealed that the staff member's claims were true. To make matters much worse, their investigation also revealed that the whistleblower who broke the news to Lance was also stealing money.

In fact, she was stealing significantly *more* money.

The checks-and-balances system within the department required two people to access county funds, but a weakness still existed. If those two people conspired to do so, they could embezzle large sums of money. That's exactly what was happening, and right under Lance's nose.

As you can imagine, the scandal quickly became public. As head of the department, the press attacked Lance. Even in his hometown newspaper, letters to the editor personally castigated Lance for his seeming involvement. Suddenly, headlines like "Treasurer facing new accusations" rained judgment on Lance's credibility and long, clean work history. Some attacks suggested he was incapable of doing anything right.

Consequently, one local attorney consistently went after Lance with a vengeance. This particular attorney had a bulldog mentality and a history of intimidating and vilifying others through the media. This attorney became Lance's nemesis and chief offender.

FAST-FORWARD SEVERAL YEARS

As Lance and I sat on the patio at Peet's Coffee Shop four years after he left office, Lance could still recall some details vividly.

"I remember one particular morning when I was walking my dog over to my Mom's house to pick up her newspaper. This was my daily routine, but that morning there was a negative headline on the front page about me. I knew this particular attorney was at it again. As I'm walking along, like never before, I noticed every newspaper in every driveway that I passed. I knew, in a matter of moments, my neighbors would be reading a negative article about me. Even though the article wasn't true, I felt so much shame. I was really feeling sorry for myself."

The all-too-public investigation and trials lasted for two years. Lance described the long, dark season like "a centipede dropping shoes" or a "continual wave crashing." People called for Lance's resignation. Multiple Board of Supervisors studies were conducted, Grand Jury hearings were held, and lots of second-guessing occurred on all sides.

Lance found himself overcome with discouragement. He suffered from the realization that several trusted people under his employment had acted negligently or with criminal intent, and several others had acted in ways that didn't consider Lance's—or the county's—best interests.

During that time, Lance said he "began to taste bitterness in the back of my mouth, and I felt my heart growing cold."

The turning point came when Lance did something extremely unusual. He began to pray for his offenders. His words say so well how freeing and healing this step can be: "It's impossible to hate someone you're praying for. So I began including these people in my evening prayers. As I moved my prayer focus away from me, then my tendency to dwell in self-pity began to decrease. Up until that point, I thought I was the star of this tragedy and everyone else was an extra. I became consciously aware that other people were involved besides me."

Lance went on to speak about the healing power he experienced in prayer: "Having the ability to talk about these enemies to God in ways that expressed my concern for their motivations, families, and uncertain futures was like having therapy with the best counselor in the universe."

But he was certain to add caution: "Now, I don't want to snow you by saying that it just took one prayer for a light to shine down from Heaven by which I could clearly see his constant love for me. Rather it was a gradual process, which may be more of a statement of how hardened and bitter my pain had left me."

PRAYING FOR YOUR ENEMIES

How about you? Do you pray for your enemy?

If you're like most people, you'd likely answer, "NO WAY!"

In fact, why would you pray for your enemy?

Praying for your enemy doesn't seem logical. After all, rational people don't help people who hurt them right?

You're supposed to hate your enemies, right?

We relate to Luke Skywalker who despised Darth Vader, Marty McFly who despised Biff Tannen, and Neo who despised Agent Smith.

Aren't we supposed to loathe the people who hurt us?

Most of us are like King David who, in one of his many moments of humanity, prayed this prayer of revenge against his enemy in Psalm 35:8-9: "May ruin overtake them by surprise. May the net they hid entangle them, may they fall into the pit, to their ruin. Then my soul will rejoice in the Lord and delight in his salvation."

Pray like that for my offender? Heck yeah! Sign me up!

But Jesus teaches an entirely different and much more difficult approach, as recorded in Matthew 5:44: "But I tell you, love your enemies and pray for those who persecute you."

Love my enemy?

Pray for the person persecuting me?

That's counter-intuitive isn't it?

That's just like Jesus!

We want to hate our enemy, but Jesus tells us to love our enemy.

We want to pray for their ruin, but Jesus teaches us to pray for their blessing.

Jesus doesn't just teach this. He personally modeled it. In fact, Luke 23:34 reveals that Jesus' first words from the cross was a prayer for his offenders: "Father, forgive them, for they do not know what they are doing."

Jesus intercedes for his offenders—even for his killers.

You will not feel like praying for the person who hurt you. It will feel awkward, forced, and unfair. So, you will have to trust Jesus and do it anyway since it was his idea to combat hurt in such a strange, hard, and ultimately rewarding way.

Let me ask you a personal question: If the perfect Son of God can love and pray for his enemies, what enemy can you have who wouldn't require your love and prayer?

Two things will happen when you pray for your enemy:

1. Your heart softens.

Pastor Daniel Hahn has wise words to this end: "I've developed a habit for people who frustrate or hurt me. My tendency is to think of them as an 'enemy' or an 'idiot.' I've noticed, the more I pray for an idiot, the less idiotic they become."

2. Those around you are impacted.

When Jesus prayed for his offenders, people nearby noticed. The thief on the cross was drawn to God after Christ's prayer. He immediately recognized Christ as the Son of God and begged for mercy. Luke 23:43 records Christ's second statement on the cross as a revealing reply to that thief: "Truly I tell you, today you will be with me in paradise."

Praying for your enemy softens your heart and reminds people around you that this life is all about him. Are you ready to begin praying for your offender?

FORGIVENESS LEADS TO FREEDOM

The Grand Jury and the District Attorney's investigation exonerated Lance of any criminal behavior. Lance told me, "I'm glad all of this happened because I grew personally, and I have learned to depend more on God. He allows us to go through stuff like that so we are reminded that this life is not all about us. Through it all, I kept anticipating blessings. I just knew God was in control, and God was going to somehow bring blessings that made him more known."

His words echo those of theologian A.W. Tozer: "When I understand that everything happening to me is to make me more Christlike, it solves a great deal of anxiety."

Lance prayed for his offenders, his heart softened, he forgave, and now he's free. Remember that it's impossible to hate someone you're praying for.

If you're ready to being praying for your offender but don't know how to start, here's a sample prayer:

"God, I've held onto this hurt long enough. Please give me the strength to overcome this and forgive [offender's name]. (Pray for any specific needs you're aware of in your offender's life). God please change [offender's] heart. Like me, [offender's name] is a sinner who needs your grace. Help him or her to know Jesus personally."

GET UNSTUCK: PUTTING IT TO WORK

1. Do you feel hatred and bitterness growing in your heart toward your offender?

2. Do you tend to focus on you? Do you dwell in self-pity? Do you feel like you're the star of this tragedy and everyone else is an extra?

3. What is the most difficult part for you as you consider praying for your offender?

4. What does it reveal about Jesus that his first act on the cross was to pray for his enemies?

5. Do you believe that God is in control? Do you believe that God can somehow use your past to make himself more known?

6. What impact would it have on those around you— friends, spouse, kids, co-workers—if you began praying for your offender?

7. Commit to pray for your offender, then share your commitment to pray with a friend who will encourage your decision.

8. Write a prayer for your offender.

9. Begin to pray daily the prayer above.

CHAPTER 7

OWN YOUR PART

*"It wasn't **my** fault. It was **their** fault. **They** hurt me. **They**
are to blame. **They** were wrong. Every objective person agrees
with me. Yet strangely, I'm the one who can't move on. Why is
that? How do I get past the stuff other people have done to me
that's turned my life upside down?"*
— Typical thoughts of a person stuck

A S I SAT IN A COFFEE SHOP PREPARING A MESSAGE ON
forgiveness, I wrote down my first point: "Own Your
Part." I paused and allowed my mind to drift back to that
day in my pastor's office several years ago. I was pretty sure
I'd already owned my part, but something inside urged me
to fully stop what I was doing and pray. So I prayed, "God,
if there is anything that I still need to own, please reveal it
to me."

Then I sat quietly, hoping for that still small voice to
stay still.

Instead, like a shark from deep within the ocean bursting into the air, one significant detail broke through the waves of my memories.

There it was. Something I had never owned. I'd never even seen it until that moment! I was immediately angry. I didn't want to own that! I thought, "After all, it was *his* fault. Why should I own anything? This doesn't feel right."

But I knew God had revealed it to me, so I paused to focus on it.

Here's what God revealed to me. When I was deciding where to plant a new church, I never included my pastor in the decision-making process. I rationalized it because our relationship had cooled, and by then he had removed himself from the process. But I should have insisted that he be a part of the location decision since it would impact him and his ministry.

Instead, I simply announced my unilateral decision to him. Deciding where to start the new church without including my pastor was a mistake. I had never owned that. Until that moment, I had never even recognized it as a mistake!

I couldn't sit in the coffee shop any longer. I left, then went on a walk where God and I had a heated exchange. I kept asking God, "Why are you just now revealing this mistake to me? I don't like feeling guilty like this. This is frustrating. It's embarrassing."

Eventually, I surrendered, then I prayed a tearful prayer of repentance. That afternoon, I owned my part of my past. I followed up with an email to my former pastor.

It was a day of healing and freedom, though that's not the end of that story. You'll get to read the rest of it in Chapter 11.

FIGHTING THE FORGIVENESS PERCENTAGE WARS

You have every right to blame someone else for what they did. After all, they were wrong. Everybody knows that. However, we tend to blame them for 100 percent of the problem. In the mental confusion that follows pain, it's easy to overlook the wrong *we've* done since our part of the past feels minor in comparison to what *they* did to us.

When I hear my kids arguing and I walk into the room, it'd be nice if they said, "Daddy, he pushed me and made me fall down. But before you punish him, I need to own my part. I was aggravating him. He pushed me, but I started it all."

Instead, they'll point a finger at a sibling and, like a tiny lawyer, make a case as to why it's entirely their sibling's fault. They don't just blame their sibling; they blame them for 100 percent of the problem—every time!

I can't blame them though. It's in my kids' DNA to blame others because I'm their dad. It's in your DNA to blame too. After all, we share the same bloodline. The blame game began with Adam and Eve in the Garden of Eden. Genesis Chapter 3 records it for us: "God asked, 'Have you eaten from the tree that I commanded you not to eat from?' Adam said, 'The woman you put here with me—she gave me some fruit from the tree, and I ate it.'

(Notice how Adam points his finger at God *and* Eve.) Then God asked Eve, 'What is this you have done?' Eve said, 'The serpent deceived me, and I ate.'"

Adam and Eve didn't just blame; they blamed others for 100 percent of their problems. Adam blamed God for creating Eve (whom he was thrilled to meet just a chapter earlier), and Adam blamed Eve for offering him the fruit. Then Eve blamed the serpent for deceiving her into eating the fruit.

Adam and Eve didn't lie. God created Eve. Eve offered the fruit to Adam. The serpent deceived Eve. But Adam and Eve were so enamored with what *others* did wrong that they didn't own any part of the problem *themselves*. Why?

Because their own sins felt minor in comparison.

As R.T. Kendall points out, "The true test of spirituality is being able *not* to point the finger!"

Remember the story of the woman caught in adultery recorded in John 8:1-11? Some religious leaders brought a woman to Jesus saying, "She's guilty. What are you gonna do about it?"

Sound familiar? Notice the 100 percent blaming?

It's an odd scenario. I don't know how these religious leaders caught a woman in the act of adultery. Somehow they physically forced her to stand before Jesus. In the heat of the moment, they were so focused on pointing their blame-filled fingers at her that they overlooked all human decency and dignity.

Scripture tells us that the Pharisees' motives were even more sinister than blaming. In John 8:4-6, they told

Jesus, "Teacher, this woman was caught in the act of adultery. In the Law, Moses commanded us to stone such women. Now what do you say?" **They were using this question as a trap, in order to have a basis for accusing him**" (emphasis added).

Not only did they want to blame this woman, they also wanted to trap Jesus so they could condemn him.

They weren't exactly others-focused fellas.

John 8:7 records Jesus' famous, oft-quoted response: "When they kept on questioning him, he straightened up and said to them, 'Let any one of you who is without sin be the first to throw a stone at her.'"

Jesus essentially says, "It's easy to focus on what this woman has done wrong. But you need to focus on what *you've* done wrong. *Own your sin*, even if it seems minor in comparison. As a sinner, you have no business focusing more on the sins of another sinner than on your own sins."

The religious accusers were stunned into silence, each one dropping their stones as they walked away. Jesus then looked at the guilty woman and reminded her to own her own sin, bluntly stating, "Go now and leave your life of sin" (John 8:11).

The Pharisees struggled with a gravitational pull we all battle. We are quick to blame others, which makes us feel innocent. The more innocent we believe we are, the more self-righteous and judgmental we become. It's a dangerous cycle. Everyone, from Adam and Eve to our own kids, blames others, which consequently works to subtly promote our own innocence.

Jesus condemns that approach. He wants you to stop blaming others and instead focus on owning your own sin.

If thinking about your past seems foggy, something may exist that you have yet to own. There is a direct link between the purity of your heart and the clarity of your thought. As Jesus attests in Matthew 5:8, "Blessed are the pure in heart, for they will see God."

To help you identify your part in past pain, it might be helpful to create a visual aid. Draw a circle that represents your past pain, then determine the percentages that represent your offender's responsibility and your responsibility.

You might even assign your offender 95 percent of the responsibility and yourself only 5 percent, but that's a better start than blaming the other person 100 percent. Adam and Eve did that and we know what resulted from that.

It's easy to focus solely on their 95 percent, but until you pause long enough to own your 5 percent, you will remain stuck!

You will never confess your sins if you blame everything on someone else. As long as you are 100 percent focused on someone else's guilt, then you're presuming that you are 100 percent innocent. That's keeping you 100 percent stuck.

And no one ever, aside from one person, is 100 percent innocent. Pastor Andy Stanley encapsulates this notion of ownership well when he writes, "To make peace with your past, you need to own your piece of the past."

Consider this truth from 1 John 1:8-10: "If we claim to be without sin, we deceive ourselves and the truth is not in us. If we confess our sins, he is faithful and just and will forgive us our sins and purify us from all unrighteousness. If we claim we have not sinned, we make him out to be a liar and his word is not in us."

There are certainly exceptions. Child abuse or an unprovoked crime can cause deep pain in which the victim has no percentage of responsibility for the offense. In those cases, victims have no part to own. Kevin's story in Chapter 4 and Erin's story in Chapter 8 are examples of such difficult circumstances, but those are rare exceptions. Most of us have something to own. For example:

- He clearly mistreated you, but as you pause and look back, maybe people had advised you to beware of him.
- She consistently demeaned and hurt you, but as you pause and look back, maybe you kept answering her texts and letting her back into your life.
- She seduced you, but as you pause and look back, maybe you stayed too long.
- He stole from you, but as you pause and look back, maybe you rushed past all of the warning signs.

Your offender is wrong for what he or she did. Owning your part of the past doesn't make your offender any less guilty, but it frees your future.

It's time to own your part, even if it's minor in comparison. This requires humility and courage, especially if you've been telling everyone (and yourself) that they were 100 percent to blame. Owning even a small percentage of the problem can be a little embarrassing, but it's a necessary step toward emotional health.

Every day that you blame the other person for 100 percent of the problem is another day you'll miss out on God's peace and purpose for your life. You can't blame your way into a better future. Blame smuggles your past into your future and steals your present all at the same time. Your best bet for a successful future and a healthier present is to own your share of the past. Take time to pause now and own your part of the past before your past keeps owning you.

GET UNSTUCK: PUTTING IT TO WORK

1. When something goes wrong, is your instinct to blame others or to own your part? How does this affect your relationships with others?

2. Can you think of a time when you've witnessed someone blame someone else—kids, students, co-workers, public figures—for 100 percent of a problem? What goes through your mind when someone does that?

3. Have you seen someone repeat mistakes from the past because that person didn't take ownership of his or her part in those mistakes?

4. What makes owning your part of the past, even if it's a little part, so difficult?

5. Ask a trusted friend if they see any part of your past that you have yet to own. Resist being defensive. Humbly thank them for loving you enough to share hard truths.

6. What is one area of your life where you haven't owned your part of the past?

7. In what ways does that prevent you from relating in a healthy way to the people in your life?

8. Draw a circle that represents your past pain, then assign percentages that represent your offender's responsibility and your responsibility.

9. Re-read 1 John 1:8-10. Continue praying that God would reveal anything in your past that you need to own. Get alone and take your time. When he reveals something, pause and own it. Don't rush. Own all of

it. Fully confess it all to God and ask for his forgiveness. This requires humility and courage, but God will provide you with that too.

CHAPTER 8

Release Their Debt

*"Getting over a painful experience is much like
crossing monkey bars. You have to let go at some
point in order to move forward."*
— C.S. Lewis

S ERENDIPITY SMILED ON WOODY WOODBURN ONE
evening when he met Erin Prewitt for the first time in
a local bookstore. What began as a brief encounter lasted
two hours and left Woody a divinely changed man.[55]

The day after they met, the twenty-four-year-old
woman who had killed Erin's husband Chris would be
sentenced in a Ventura, California courtroom. Chris, a
beloved educator, had been on a marathon-training run
when he was struck and killed by a woman driving under
the influence of marijuana and Xanax.

Despite the senseless act that made Erin a widow and
left her seven-year-old daughter fatherless, Erin shared
with Woody what she would tell the judge the next day:
Chris would forgive, therefore she would too. Even then,

Erin anticipated receiving criticism for offering forgiveness to the defendant at the sentencing.

From nearly the moment she received the tragic news of her husband's death, Erin decided to grant forgiveness for many reasons. First, she chose to forgive for her own healing, recognizing the wisdom of Nelson Mandela: "As I walked out the door toward the gate that would lead to my freedom, I knew if I didn't leave my bitterness and hatred behind, I'd still be in prison."

Also, she hoped to plant the rich fruit of strength in her daughter. Erin felt a responsibility to set the tone for the rest of her family and friends, as well as the community at large. Mark Twain wrote, "Forgiveness is the fragrance that the violet sheds on the heel that has crushed it." Erin Prewitt is a human violet, crushed by a heel of tragedy, yet already blooming again.

On that next day, June 27, 2014 to be exact, the courtroom was packed. On one side sat those supporting the defendant. On the other side sat those supporting the Prewitt family. While an aisle separated the two groups, you couldn't help but notice that the sides were also separated by distinctly different skin color. All of these people lived in the same town and were members of the same community, but they looked like they were from two different worlds. There were extra deputies present because of a concern that someone from either side might act out violently.

As Erin gave voice to her victim impact statement, everyone was shocked, then touched. She wanted to make it clear that she forgave the defendant, that she harbored no ill will toward her, and that she wanted the best for her and her family. Erin spoke of her own strong belief in God, letting everyone know that her recently deceased husband held the same belief.

Her simple, honest words of forgiveness affected the entire courtroom. Seasoned sheriff's deputies were moved to tears. The court clerk openly sobbed. The defense attorney could barely compose himself enough to speak. The judge felt compelled to excuse himself for thirty minutes to reign in his emotions.

During a recess, Erin approached the defendant and hugged her in the middle of the courtroom. They held their embrace. One of the attorneys in the room said, "The act of extending God's grace to another human being instantaneously affected all those present. I will remember this day as one of the most powerful experiences I have witnessed in a courtroom or anywhere else."

Woody was one of those profoundly impacted by that experience because he'd suffered a similar, life-altering tragedy at the hands of an intoxicated driver eleven years prior. Though Woody had survived the high-speed collision, he'd suffered permanent injury. His bitterness at the drunken driver had also been permanent.

But his chance (God-ordained) encounter with Erin changed that. After hearing her story, Woody firmly decided, "If she can forgive, how can I not forgive? She decided to release the debt. So will I."

THE DEBT-RELEASE DECISION

Someone did something to you.

Someone took something from you.

Someone owes you something.

Maybe they took your first marriage, your reputation, your financial security, your career, your self-esteem, or your dream. Whatever they took, they created a debt. Here's a hard truth you likely already know somewhere down deep: They aren't going to pay you back. They probably *can't* pay you back.

Mike didn't pay Lori back. Phil's dad couldn't pay Phil back. Jason couldn't pay Kevin back. Lance couldn't be paid back. Erin couldn't be paid back. Woody couldn't be paid back. Your offender won't pay you back.

Here's a difficult question: how far into your future will you carry the pain from your past? A week? A month? A year? Eleven years, like Woody?

In Chapter 2 I shared "Fourteen Things Forgiveness is Not." Now, I want to share my definition of forgiveness. Forgiveness is deciding to release the other person's debt to you. That's what God did for us. That's what you can do for your offender. The key word in that definition is *deciding*. It's a decision that you are capable of making.

They created the debt. That wasn't your decision. But it is your decision to carry or release their debt.

Have you ever known someone who had it all together? They have a happy marriage, well-behaved kids, a successful career, and they even have a perfect set of teeth. Then one day you discover they've experienced a deep hurt in their past. You think, "I would never have guessed they'd experienced anything like that."

When that happens, I always ask that person, "How did you overcome that hurt and become such a happy person?" Every single person begins to answer that question the same way: "Well, I just decided . . ."

I *decided*. They made a decision.

These stories often happen in the lives of people I know, especially when I take the time to discover who they are beyond a typical, surface-level friendship. By all appearances, this one friend in particular has a wrinkle-free life. He's a successful attorney with a great marriage and fantastic kids. However, I knew about a deeply painful season in his past. So, as I prepared to write this chapter, I met him for coffee and asked, "How could you have experienced such a deep hurt and yet be such a positive and generous person now?"

He said, "When I felt my heart hardening, I just *decided* that I didn't want to become a bitter person and it was time to do something."

There's that word again. He *decided*.

That's where forgiveness begins. You decide!

Imagine in a few months from now someone saying to you, "I would have never guessed that you had ever experienced anything like the hurt you've experienced. You are such a positive and generous person. How did you overcome that difficult hurt in your life?"

You could say to them, "Well, I just *decided*."

Scripture teaches that releasing the other person's debt begins with a decision. In Ephesians 4:26-32, the Apostle Paul said, "In your anger do not sin . . ." Paul points out that anger and sin are two different things. You can be angry and not sin. Or, you can be angry and sin. What's the difference? Paul explains, "In your anger do not sin: Do not let the sun go down while you are still angry." Anger becomes sin when you hold on to it for too long. Paul says that initial anger is appropriate, but smuggling it into our future is sinful.

I don't believe Paul is literally suggesting that *all* deep hurts must be forgiven before the end of the day. But Paul does say carrying your anger into the future, at some point, becomes sin. Ask yourself, "For how many more sunsets will I carry the pain of my past?" According to Paul, the decision is yours.

Holding on to past pain is like the little boy at the park sitting on a bench in obvious pain. A man walked by and noticed the boy was in pain, so he asked what was wrong.

The boy answered, "I'm sitting on a bumble bee."

"Then why don't you get up?"

"Because I figure I'm hurting him more than he's hurting me!"

Releasing debt requires you to decide to get off the park bench.

Why is holding on to your anger such a big deal? In Ephesians 4:26, Paul goes on to say, " . . . and do not give the devil a foothold."

Carrying your grudge is like giving Satan a rent-free room in your heart. Remember, Satan's goal is to deform your heart into something hard and cold. Your grudge becomes a basecamp where Satan can launch relentless attacks intended to harden your heart. Carrying a grudge significantly increases the chances of his success. It's extremely dangerous to carry a grudge.

But how do you release their debt? In Ephesians 4:31-32, Paul says, *"Get rid of all bitterness, rage and anger, brawling and slander, along with every form of malice. Be kind and compassionate to one another, forgiving each other, just as in Christ God forgave you."*

In other words, *decide!*

THE POWER TO DECIDE

You may be thinking, "I do want to get rid of this bitterness and anger, but I don't I have it in me to release their debt." The good news is that your ability to release their debt doesn't come from you; it comes from Jesus. When releasing their debt seems like it will cost you more than you think you have, the cross says it doesn't. Apart from Jesus you can do nothing (John 15:5).

When it comes to their debt, Jesus paid it all. Their debt left a crimson stain, but he will wash it white as snow. The cross is the moment when the Messiah hand-delivered the power to release all debt. This is the axis of Christianity. The cross reveals two monumental truths: sin is a big deal, but grace is bigger.

Never allow your offender's offense to overshadow God's grace.

Recall Colossians 2:13-15: "When you were dead in your sins and in the uncircumcision of your flesh, God made you alive with Christ. He forgave us all our sins, having canceled the charge of our legal indebtedness, which stood against us and condemned us; he has taken it away, nailing it to the cross. And having disarmed the powers and authorities, he made a public spectacle of them, triumphing over them by the cross."

Frederick Buechner speaks to the treacherous allure of holding on to a debt: "Of all the deadly sins, resentment appears to be the most fun. To lick your wounds and savor the pain you will give back is in many ways a feast fit for a king. But then it turns out that what you are eating at the banquet of bitterness is your own heart. The skeleton at the feast is you. You start out holding a grudge, but in the end the grudge holds you."

You cannot receive God's grace while clinging to a grudge. Allow me to restate C.S. Lewis' insightful words: "Getting over a painful experience is much like crossing monkey bars. You have to let go at some point in order to move forward." When we let go of the "monkey bars" of our pain, what should we reach for?

Let's join Paul when he said, "I'm not saying that I have this all together, that I have it made. But I am well on my way, **reaching out for Christ**, who has so wondrously reached out for me. Friends, don't get me wrong: By no means do I count myself an expert in all of this, but I've got my eye on the goal, where God is beckoning us onward—to Jesus. I'm off and running, and I'm not turning back" (Philippians 3:12-14, *The Message*, emphasis added).

Are you ready to release the debt? If so, here's a sample prayer. For assistance in filling in the blanks, refer to the work you did in Chapter 4 on identifying the injustice, damage, and consequences.

Heavenly Father, (OFFENDER) injured me by (INJUSTICE). As a result, I experienced (DAMAGE) and (CONSEQUENCES). I have held this debt long enough. I choose to release this debt. (OFFENDER) doesn't owe me anymore. Just as you released my debt, I release (OFFENDER)'s debt.

Initially, you may need to repeat this prayer several times a day. Then you may need to repeat it daily for several weeks. No matter how often you pray, make a decision to release the debt—for good.

CREATE A FORGIVENESS MEMORY

It may help to mark your decision by doing something tangible and creating a forgiveness memory. You'll find some ideas at the end of this chapter, but first, a fascinating illustration on just what, precisely, a forgiveness memory is.

I once went on a three-day hike with some friends to the bottom of the Grand Canyon. On our way down the South Kaibab Trail, we crossed paths with a man from London. We began talking and he revealed that he had flown all the way across the Atlantic Ocean so he could forgive someone and "leave it all at the bottom of the canyon."

Why did he choose such a demanding and time-consuming measure? He saw the value of creating a tangible forgiveness memory.

In the days following our meeting, I'm sure this fellow hiker will be tempted to replay his past hurt. When that happens, I envision a smile creeping across his face as he remembers releasing his hurt once and for all at the bottom of the Grand Canyon instead of replaying the hurt itself. That's a much better memory!

GET UNSTUCK: PUTTING IT TO WORK

1. Have you ever met someone with a "wrinkle-free" life, but discovered something surprisingly difficult about their past and thought, "No one would have ever guessed you'd gone through that?" From what you know, describe how that person became who they are because of, or despite, their past pain.

2. Have you ever known someone who refused to release his or her past? How did this impact their outlook on life?

3. Do you recognize that carrying a grudge only hurts you?

4. How would your life be better if you released the other person's debt?

5. Forgiveness does not happen in isolation. Who will benefit when you release the debt? How will they benefit?

6. Do you know someone who has endured a deep pain, but has released his or her grudge? Could you invite them to help you release your grudge?

7. Read these passages to discover what God thinks about revenge: Ezekiel 25:15-17, Romans 12:14-21, and 1 Peter 3:8-17.

8. Write some good things you've received that you didn't deserve.

9. Would your suffering be worthwhile if it helped transform even one person in this world?

10. Write the possible reasons God could have allowed you to endure specific pain in your life. For exam-

ple, to help others who will endure similar pain, to increase my dependence upon God, to discover the depth and beauty of forgiveness, etc.

11. Share your prayers to release the debt with a trusted friend, asking them to pray that you remain surrendered.

12. If you're struggling to release the debt, take time to read about others who have been deeply hurt and learned how to release the debt. Read the story of Joseph in Genesis 37-50. Read *As We Forgive: Stories of Reconciliation from Rwanda* by Catherine Claire Larson.

13. Honestly accept the fact that your offender will not pay you back.

14. Make a list of people who have forgiven deep hurts.

15. What pain have some of those heroes endured? What debts have they omitted?

16. Spend time listing your sins and thanking God for releasing your debt through Jesus' death on the cross.

17. Commit to praying a prayer like this:
Heavenly Father, (OFFENDER) injured me by (INJUSTICE). As a result, I experienced (DAMAGE) and (CONSEQUENCES). I have held this debt long enough. I choose to release this debt. (OFFENDER) doesn't owe me anymore. Just as you released my debt, I release (OFFENDER)'s debt.

18. Stop reliving the pain by releasing the debt.

Battle memories of the past with Scripture. Memorize Colossians 2:13-15.

Mark your decision by creating a forgiveness memory.

FORGIVENESS MEMORY IDEAS:

Write a letter listing everything your offender did, then forgive them and burn the letter.

Make a symbol (cross, ring, quilt, painting, etc.) that becomes a constant reminder of your decision to forgive.

Throw yourself a forgiveness party. Invite some friends and celebrate forgiveness (yours, theirs, and God's). Take pictures to remind you of your decision.

CHAPTER 9

REWRITE YOUR STORY

"A good pen . . . can turn tragedy into hope and victory."
— Nelson Mandela

ONE OF THE MOST OVERLOOKED FACTORS IN DETERmining God's plan for your life is past hurts you've overcome. Since purpose usually comes out of struggles, not strengths, you should pay close attention to what you've learned in the school of hard knocks.

Satan loves to hear you casually reference your past because he knows that every time you tell what happened, you're navigating landmines that could trigger some ugly emotional explosions.

In other words, if you haven't rewritten your story, your story is a liability. However, God specializes in converting pain into purpose. That's what the Apostle Paul was talking about in Philippians 1:12 when he said, "Now I want you to know, brothers, that what has happened to me has really served to advance the gospel."

Instead of a liability, your story can become a strength.

In Chapter 3, you've stopped telling your story as a victim.

Now it's time to intentionally rewrite it.

WATERFALL OR BUSTED CHAINS?

On one Christmas vacation, our family went to Yosemite National Park. Our first night was both magical and disastrous. Due to heavy snow, every vehicle had to have snow chains before entering the park. While driving to the ski lodge, our first set of brand new snow chains broke, and our vehicle slid off the road. We were stuck in ice and snow.

A professional came to the scene and concluded that our snow chains were inadequate for those winter conditions, so he installed a brand new set of $300, high-end snow chains that were "guaranteed for life."

I kept wondering, "So what conditions were our *snow*-chains equipped for?"

Later that day, we drove back down the mountain to where there wasn't as much snow. I pulled over to remove the chains. As I got out of our Suburban and looked around, I noticed the jaw-dropping beauty of Bridal Falls. The powerful rush of such a winter waterfall was breathtaking. I stood there and soaked in the majesty of my Creator. Then I got back to the task.

It was getting dark, and as I positioned myself onto the wet asphalt underneath our muddy vehicle, I quickly realized there was another problem. I couldn't get the stinkin' snow-chains off! Since I don't have a mechanical bone in my body, I kept re-reading the instructions and giving it another try, but those suckers weren't coming off! To make matters worse, when we called the company that had installed the chains only two hours earlier, no one answered. So we called a different company.

While we waited, Ginger and the kids grabbed sleds from the back of the Suburban and began playing in the snow. I was in no mood for fun. Honestly, I was flat-out mad. (I may be a pastor, but my sanctification has a ways to go.) When our rescuer arrived, he discovered that the chains had been installed backwards, making them impossible to remove! What? We had to pay him $100 to cut off our $300, "life-time guarantee" chains.

That's about the same time we decided to park the Suburban and take the bus the next day. At the cabin that night, Ginger decided to tell the story of our day by posting pictures on social media. I still wasn't in the mood, so she was going to choose what pictures to share. Whichever pictures she chose would tell our story.

Now, she could've selected only pictures of tow-trucks, tire-chain receipts, and broken tire-chains. Believe me, I had those pictures! Those pictures alone would have made our day look completely disastrous.

Or she could've only selected the photos that displayed the silent beauty of falling snow, snow-capped mountains, moonlit waterfalls, and our kids playing with their sleds in the snow. She had those pictures! Those pictures alone would have made our day look magical and problem-free.

However, our day was both magical and disastrous. So, my wife chose a couple pictures that revealed the pain and a couple that revealed the beauty of our day, with captions like, "Snow chains = $300, Snow chains removed = $100, Magnificent beauty and memories with kids in the snow = priceless."

I argued that it was anything but priceless, but I may have been letting my emotions lead at that point.

What's the point of my story?

Your rewritten story doesn't have to ignore your pain.

But it's critical to find meaning in your pain. Finding meaning is different than simply being positive. Finding meaning in suffering allows you to see how you have grown from a difficult experience without calling that experience good.

Dr. Victor Frankl, a psychiatrist once held in a World War II concentration camp, found that the only people who were not emotionally destroyed by that horrific experience were those who found meaning in the atrocity. Joy arrives when meaning is found in suffering.

As I think back on that day in Yosemite, it's now a positive memory. The experience of this transplanted Texan installing snow chains, sliding off the road, spinning my tires, waiting on tow trucks, and paying ridiculously high charges was initially painful. But knowing I pushed through it all so that our family could create meaningful memories eventually brought me joy.

Sustaining forgiveness will require you to choose the pictures that reveal your pain, your Creator's hand, and your story's hope. Rewriting your story will knock Satan to his knees.

God specializes in redeeming past pain! I've personally witnessed and experienced that truth. The ministry experiences I am now enjoying are a direct result my past hurt. This book is a result of my past pain. God loves to redeem! You may even inspire someone as they watch you go through this forgiveness process. Either way, God wants you to leverage your past for his glory.

Remember good ol' "thorn in the flesh" Paul? When referencing how God loves to leverage a difficult past, in *The Message* translation of 2 Corinthians 1:4, Paul says, "He comes alongside us when we go through hard times, and before you know it, he brings us alongside someone else who is going through hard times so that we can be there for that person just as God was there for us."

When it comes to finding meaning in suffering, consider these three questions:

- Would my suffering be worthwhile if it helped transform another person?
- What good has already come from my suffering?
- What good could come from my suffering?

After being betrayed, Joseph rewrote his story as recorded in Genesis 50:20: "You intended to harm me, but God intended it for good to accomplish what is now being done, the saving of many lives." Every time you hear yourself telling a painful story about your past, stop and discover if you're about to paint your pain as purposeless or with careful brushstrokes of meaning and hope.

HOW DID JESUS REWRITE HIS STORY?

Jesus *always* told his story carefully. Listen in as he describes the moments just before his crucifixion: "I offered my back to those who beat me, my cheeks to those who pulled out my beard; I did not hide my face from mocking and spitting. Because the Sovereign Lord helps me, I will not be disgraced. Therefore have I set my face like a flint, and I know I will not be put to shame. He who vindicates me is near" (Isaiah 50:6-8a).

There's not a hint of Jesus being a victim, is there? Instead, he tells his story with purpose, perspective, and hope. These prophetic words of the Messiah are recorded in Isaiah 50 and referenced again by Luke in his Gospel.

Why does Jesus tell his story that way?

He answers that question in Isaiah 50:4, "The Sovereign Lord has given me a **well-instructed tongue**" (emphasis added). God the Father wanted Jesus to tell an intentional story.

God wants you to tell an intentional story!

When you tell your story, do you have a well-instructed tongue?

You can, and you should.

Satan wants you to tell your story casually.

God wants you to tell your story intentionally.

REWRITE YOUR STORY WITH H.O.P.E.

It's time for you to rewrite your story. But how? Here's a tool that can help you. The H.O.P.E. tool will help you rewrite your story in only four sentences. I'll describe the four sentences, then illustrate the H.O.P.E. tool by comparing my personal "before" and "after" stories.

First, here are the four sentences.

H: Write your "hope" sentence.

This is the personal and specific hope you originally held before your hurt.

O: Write your "observe" sentence.

You observe that every hope includes the possibility of failure.

P: Write your "positive" sentence.

You recognize some of the positive things God has produced in your life as result of your pain.

E: Write your "enduring" sentence.

Re-establish your enduring goals and values.

Here's my "before" story:

God called me to plant a church, and my pastor wouldn't support me. His lack of support negatively impacted my church-planting efforts. I don't know why God would allow this, and I'm struggling to forgive my former pastor.

Can you sense the hopelessness and see my tendency to play the blame game? Fred Luskin said, "When we blame another person for how we feel, we grant them the power to regulate our emotions."

Satan wanted me to stick with that story. It's full of bitterness seeds that produce destructive emotions. This story would have left me completely vulnerable to Satan's fatal uppercut.

When you settle for describing what happened, you're not using a well-instructed tongue. As Fred Luskin also points out, "The primary purpose of any story you tell is to help you place what happened in context. The secondary purpose is to describe what happened."

I *decided* (there's that word again) to craft my story using the four sentences of the H.O.P.E. tool. Here is my rewritten story that I currently tell:

Hope: I had hoped my pastor would fully support our church-planting effort.

Observe: Though he didn't support me, many church planters lack the support of their former pastors.

Positive: As a result of that painful season, God grew my faith, grew the faith of others, and has now increased my ministry opportunities.

Enduring: I am learning that mountaintops and valleys are both part of the adventurous life for Christ that I am continuing to pursue.

Remember Lori in Chapter 3?

Her rewritten story is:

Hope: "I had hoped for a faithful, life-long marriage."

Observe: "However, like many people, I experienced a divorce."

Positive: "God faithfully provided for my family and me, and I grew spiritually through that season."

Enduring: "I now enjoy a wonderful marriage to a godly man and am grateful that God is using my experience to encourage others."

After forgiving his Dad, here's Phil's rewritten story:

Hope: "I wanted my Mom and Dad to both enjoy a long, healthy life together."

Observe: "Though my Mom's death was too soon, I recognize that death is a difficult but inevitable reality for everyone."

Positive: "Through all of this, God has deepened my faith as I've chosen to rely more upon him."

Enduring: "I am learning to forgive more quickly and hope to inspire my wife, kids, and others to live a life of forgiveness."

After forgiving Jason, here's Kevin's rewritten story:

Hope: "I loved athletics and hoped to live a physically active life."

Observe: "However, this world is full of broken people, which is why I'm a quadriplegic.

Positive: "I believe I am less physically active, but more spiritually alive due to my injury."

Enduring: "God is using my injury and my forgiveness to inspire others, and this tragic event changed the course of my family's life in a positive way."

Satan wants to knock you out. His greatest weapon is your past pain. Rewriting your story will help you elevate purpose over your pain. With that in mind, will you develop a well-instructed tongue? Will you rewrite your story?

GET UNSTUCK: PUTTING IT TO WORK

1. Rewrite your story with the four-sentence H.O.P.E. tool:

H: Write your "hope" sentence.

This is the personal and specific hope you originally held before your hurt.

O: Write your "observe" sentence.

You observe that every hope includes the possibility of failure.

P: Write your "positive" sentence.

You recognize some of the positive things God has produced in your life as result of your pain.

E: Write your "enduring" sentence.

Re-establish your enduring goals and values.

2. Practice sharing your new, rewritten story with several friends.

CHAPTER 10

THE DIRTY LITTLE SECRET
ABOUT FORGIVENESS

*"I don't want to be at the mercy of my emotions.
I want to use them, to enjoy them, and to dominate them."*
— Oscar Wilde

CONFESSION: I NEVER FELT LIKE FORGIVING.
You'll never feel like forgiving either, at least not long enough to see it through. Your grudge will feel more like a guilty pleasure. You'll fantasize about saying just the right things at just the right time to make your enemy seem small and yourself seem better in front of just the right people.

Just as true love is not an emotion but a choice, forgiveness is not an emotion; it's a choice. But your feelings will play a major role in your forgiveness process. And, that should scare you!

The dirty little secret about forgiveness is that your feelings will try to sabotage you. Guaranteed.

So what should you do?

Well, don't do what I did.

THE FEELINGS THAT FAILED ME

My nine-year-old daughter's voice revealed her concern, "Daddy, are you okay?"

She spoke those caring words about two years after the hurt I wrote about in the first chapter. I was sitting in my recliner, physically frozen and emotionally numb. "Yeah, I'm okay," I lied. I didn't want her to know anything about the dark, internal battle raging inside of me. For the first time in my life, I was facing an extended funk. I don't know if it was depression, but I just couldn't shake it.

Have you ever battled that? If you have, you know it's exhausting. Some days start off fine. But then, without notice, a fog rolls in and pulls you into an emotional sinkhole. Winston Churchill struggled with depression and referred to it as his "personal black dog." For me, it was more like a gray fog. I thought I was showing strength by ignoring my emotions.

Turns out that's a great recipe for a low-level, long-lasting emotional funk.

Do you know that God is interested in how you feel?

When we feel emotions, we typically react in one of two ways: by allowing an emotion to control us or by altogether ignoring it. Which do you tend to do? You probably know your tendency.

Scripture teaches a better way. Psalm 51:6 says, "Behold, you delight in truth in the inward being, and you teach me wisdom in the secret heart."

Chip Dodd expounds, "Whenever you lack awareness of your heart, less room exists for God." When you understand your feelings, you can surrender more of yourself to God. It all starts in your heart. Matthew 18:35 tells us that the heart produces forgiveness as well as emotions. Consequently, ignoring your heart means ignoring what it can produce.

Do you know that your emotions try to tell you something important?

Do you know that listening to your heart is a spiritual discipline?

Do you know that listening to your heart's emotions is part of the forgiveness process?

I didn't.

Emotions are great indicators, but terrible leaders. Emotions are friends, not decision-makers. Sometimes we think we should feel differently before we act differently. That puts our emotions in charge. Instead, truth should lead.

A healthier pattern is to start with truth, followed by thinking, followed by actions, followed by feelings. Truth > Thoughts > Actions > Feelings. You may rarely feel like doing the right thing. That's why you may say things like, "I don't feel like forgiving them."

God doesn't tell us how to feel. Instead, he tells us how to think and act, knowing our feelings will follow. Your emotions shouldn't lead, but they shouldn't be ignored either. God gave you your emotions, and they are internal indicators that communicate something important. It's possible to bypass your feelings, but they provide crucial information revealing what you value and what needs your attention. If you ignore your emotions, you'll miss an important message. Chip Dodd points out, "There are no bad emotions—only good ones. Every one of these emotions is a tool that allow us to get through a tragedy and live fully despite the brokenness among us."

Ignoring your heart but demanding that it produces forgiveness is like ignoring the warning lights on your car's dashboard but expecting it to drive you across the country. Your heart patiently says, "When you're ready to listen, I'm ready to talk." Your emotions reveal how your injustice is impacting your heart.

About a third of the Psalms are psalms of lament and can be broken into three broad categories:

- Hurt caused the Psalmist to react with *anger* in Psalm 13, 18, 31, 50, 55, 59, 73, 79, and 137.
- Crises—unexpected and frightening circumstances that threaten our well-being—caused the Psalmist to respond with *fear* in Psalm 18, 28, 46, 88, 107, and 144.
- Difficulties—relentless problems that drag on and sap energy and joy— caused the Psalmist to experience extended *discouragement* in Psalm 10, 13, 22, 42, 73, 77, 88, and 107.

After I walked out of my Pastor's office that fateful day, I began a three-year emotional roller coaster that I had never before experienced. In fact, my own emotional journey mirrored the Psalmist. At first, I was primarily angry because my friend hurt me deeply. A few weeks later, as the reality of my new circumstances sank in (change of job and social circle), it felt more like a crisis and my primary emotion transitioned from anger to fear. Two years later, when my adventure felt more like relentless difficulties, my primary emotion transitioned from fear to discouragement.

As a result of my discouragement, I began to visit and benefit from a counselor for the first time in my life. Her insight began to provide perspective on my problem and see that I was making this more tragic than it really was. My counselor encouraged me to see that my circumstances were unique but my pain and emotional reactions were normal.

I needed to learn how to handle my emotions going forward in a more healthy way. Then I read Chip Dodd's book, *The Voice of the Heart*, which revealed three healthy responses to emotions. These three responses have allowed me to pay attention to my emotions without allowing them to lead.

After identifying the emotions that you're feeling (it may help to refer back to the emotions chart in Chapter 4), consider these three healthy responses:

Response #1: Allow yourself to feel fully.

Don't just identify the feeling. Take the time to allow yourself to fully feel it. This is harder for those of us who tend to ignore (or stuff) our feelings. But this is an investment worth making. The first step may be as simple as increasing your emotional vocabulary. It may help to print out the list of emotions in Chapter 4 and put it on your refrigerator door as a reminder.

Response #2: Honestly describe what you feel.

Describing what you feel helps you fully feel it and become more aware of what's going on inside your heart. God is interested in what's going on there. Like throwing a baseball, this is a skill that can be developed. Over time, you'll identify and describe your feelings more quickly and effectively.

Response #3: Surrender control of that feeling to God.

You now have something specific to surrender to God in prayer. This will likely be a process that needs to be repeated. Repeated prayers of surrender help to loosen the grip of your emotion.

For me, when I'm talking to God, part of my prayer discusses what I'm feeling. It's helpful for me to talk through these three responses. In other words, I identify what I'm feeling, and then I describe it to him. I am often embarrassed that I'm feeling certain emotions like jealousy, anger, or insecurity, but it's important for me to approach him honestly. Besides, God already knows what I'm feeling. Then I surrender control of that feeling to God. This is always so freeing for me, and it creates a more intimate relationship between God and me.

Afterwards, God often reveals something (usually a lie that I've been believing) behind my emotion that I hadn't seen before. That must be what the Psalmist described in Psalm 51:6 when he said, "Behold, you delight in truth in the inward being, and you teach me wisdom in the secret heart."

The dirty little secret of forgiveness is that your emotions will try to sabotage you. You will not feel like forgiving the person who hurt you. Don't let your emotions lead, but don't ignore them either. *Decide* to lead your emotions throughout the process. Identify your feelings, allow yourself to fully feel and describe them, then surrender control of those feelings to God.

Why is this so important? The heart is where all the magic happens.

Your heart is a launching pad for forgiveness.

Proverbs 4:23 reminds us of this oft-forgotten fact: "Above all else, guard your heart, for everything you do flows from it."

It's easy to read in a book, but winning the war against your emotions is one of the hardest yet most rewarding steps you can take toward forgiving your offender.

In fact, once you've chosen to forgive despite your sometimes misleading feelings, you'll discover something surprising, godly, and freeing.

You're no longer stuck.

GET UNSTUCK: PUTTING IT TO WORK

1. Identify your emotions.
2. After identifying your emotions, do three things:
   - Allow yourself to feel fully.
   - Honestly describe what you feel.
   - Surrender control of that feeling to God.
3. Journal your emotions and your responses. Since this is a process, recording your emotional journey is helpful.

CHAPTER 11

Seek Reconciliation

*"[Reconciliation] is a risky undertaking, but in the end it
is worthwhile, because in the end only an honest confrontation
with reality can bring real healing."*
— Desmond Tutu

THE GREAT PARADOX OF HUMAN RELATIONSHIPS IS
that we are created to heal each other from the hurts
we inflict on one other. In this chapter, I'll share my
personal journey of reconciling with my former pastor. I
like to think of reconciliation as the cherry on top of the
forgiveness sundae, and you'll soon see why. But first, let
me mention one caution.

RECONCILIATION IS NOT REQUIRED

You can experience complete forgiveness *without*
reconciliation. Ideally, you'll forgive your offender, your
offender will forgive you, and then you both reconcile. That
is the way God intends.

But that option is not entirely up to you. In certain circumstances, reconciliation may not be possible or even recommended. Reconciliation may not be an option for you if:

- Your offender is abusive and reconciling would cause further injury.
- Your offender has died.
- Your offender does not want to reconcile.
- Your offender is unrepentant.

It only takes one person to forgive, but it takes two people to reconcile. Reconciliation is not always appropriate. The good news is that *you* can complete the forgiveness process without reconciliation.

In Romans 12:18, the Apostle Paul reminds us, "If it is possible, **as far as it depends on you**, live at peace with everyone" (emphasis added).

You are only responsible for your behavior. When it comes to living at peace with others, do your part. But your offender also has a part. If you are the only one making the effort toward reconciliation, then it's unlikely to happen. If they are unwilling to do their part, reconciliation is not required.

But if reconciliation *is* a possibility, what steps can a person take to reconcile with someone who's hurt them so deeply?

SIX SIMPLE AND EFFECTIVE GUIDELINES FOR RECONCILIATION

After reading that caution, if you're ready to reconcile, I recommend these six guidelines for your reconciliation process:

Guideline #1: Depend on God

Do you remember why Jacob battled an angel? After a twenty-year separation, Jacob was about to attempt reconciliation with Esau. So, Jacob wrestled with an angel demanding God's blessing for what he was about to do. As Genesis 32:26 tells the story, "Then the man said, 'Let me go, for it is daybreak.' But Jacob replied, **'I will not let you go unless you bless me'**" (emphasis added). Despite his wisdom and wealth, Jacob was dependent upon God. Start and continue with prayer, maintaining a dependent heart throughout the reconciliation process.

Guideline #2: Aim for Peace

In Romans 12:18, the Apostle Paul reminds us, "If it is possible, as far as it depends on you, **live at peace with everyone**" (emphasis added). The goal of reconciliation is peace. Peace is much more attainable than trying to fully restore a broken relationship back to where it was. Maybe you want to reconcile with a parent, child, former spouse, former boss, or former friend. A deeper relationship may eventually develop, but establish the goal of restoring peace instead of bowing under the pressure of feeling the need to restore a friendship.

Guideline #3: Seek to Understand

Seek to understand the other person's perspective instead of only presenting and believing your side of the story. Proverbs 18:13 reads, "To answer before listening—that is folly and shame."

Resist the urge to present your case or defend yourself. Instead, quietly listen, then restate the other person's perspective. Ask them if you're understanding their perspective accurately. Real progress can be made when *they* agree that you understand *their* perspective. St. Francis of Assisi offers wise words on this point too: "Seek first to understand, then to be understood."

Guideline #4: Don't Accuse

When appropriate, share your perspective, but avoid finger-pointing or accusations. One rule-of-thumb is to use "I" statements instead of "you" statements. For example, instead of saying, "You betrayed me," you could say, "I felt betrayed." "I" statements allow the other person to respond without feeling defensive. Use "I" statements to help you share honestly but without accusations.

Guideline #5: Apologize Early

Early on in the process of reconciliation, find something about which you can offer regret or an apology. This helps reveal your humility and commitment to true reconciliation. An early apology or regret will go a long way toward rebuilding trust in this tenuous process. James 5:16 reads, "Therefore confess your sins to each other and pray for each other so that you may be healed. The prayer of a righteous person is powerful and effective."

Guideline #6: One Issue at a Time

Deal with one issue at a time. There may be one major issue of disagreement. However, most broken relationships include many smaller issues of disagreement. In order to accomplish Guideline #3, *Seek to Understand*, you'll need to address each issue individually. Make sure the other person feels completely heard and understood on each issue before moving on to the next one.

MY STORY OF RECONCILIATION

My family and I moved to Ventura, California in 2011. As I walked barefoot in my backyard, I spoke with a long-time friend from West Texas. He asked, "Did you guys ever reconcile?"

I thought, "Reconcile? You're my friend. You know exactly what he did! Why would you even ask that?"

Then he said, "It just seems like the Bible tells us to keep short accounts."

Sometimes I wish my friends had still small voices too, stress on *still*.

I agreed with him, but secretly decided I knew things he didn't understand.

We hung up. In the silence that followed, my quiet inner voice began to speak. I sensed the Holy Spirit asking me, "So what's your answer? Why haven't you reconciled?"

I took a deep breath and decided that it had been long enough. I was about to re-enter my past and take a journey that scared me to death. I grabbed my laptop and wrote an email to my former friend and pastor.

I didn't want to mess this up, so I asked my wife and another friend to read it before I sent the email. I asked my former pastor if he would consider reconciling. If he said "no," which I fully expected, I could at least have a clear conscience the next time someone would ask me, "Did you guys ever reconcile?"

My email wasn't poignant or witty. I recalled a fun, shared memory, then I simply asked, "I don't know what reconciliation between us would look like, but would you be willing to consider it?"

The next day I was shocked when my former friend and pastor said, "Yes." I felt like a dog that had been chasing a car tire and finally caught it. "Oh crap," I thought. "Now what? I have no idea how to walk through a reconciliation process."

Fortunately, God was way ahead of me. My Executive Pastor Jack Monroe had specific training and experience in helping people reconcile with each other. I invited him into the reconciliation process, and he was happy to help.

After exchanging dozens of emails with my former friend and pastor and working through all of our major issues, we came to a place where we either agreed upon our issues or at least understood the other person's thinking.

More shocking to me than the fact that he was open to reconciliation was the biggest discovery I made during the reconciliation process.

I wasn't as innocent as I thought I was.

During our email exchanges, I found myself expressing regret and asking for forgiveness much more than I ever anticipated. Honestly, it frustrated me a little. Okay, it frustrated me a lot! When I was carrying my grudge, the issues were black and white. Suddenly, they appeared gray.

Now, there are many painful situations that are clearly one-sided. For example, child abuse is completely unprovoked. So your situation may be an exception. However, as pastor and author John Ortberg has said, "as a general rule, where there is hurt, I am both the victim of and the agent of wrongdoing. In most relationships where deep pain is involved, I must both forgive and seek forgiveness."

For years, I viewed myself as an innocent lamb and my offender as a mean wolf. But I was reminded that we were two equally broken people who experienced an equally deep hurt. That surprised me. I was so focused on *my* hurt that I didn't think or care about any hurt *I* caused. But a softened heart allowed me to see that I am just as capable of good and evil as my offender is.

So is your offender.

So are you.

But thankfully that's not the end of our story.

Reconciliation restored peace. Despite the years that had passed, it was a significant healing in my life, a reminder that it's never too late to reconcile.

Soon after our reconciliation, I interviewed my former pastor for my blog. Below, you'll find my questions and his honest answers:

I was not only your Associate Pastor for twelve years, but we were pretty close friends weren't we?

"We met in 1994 when my family first moved to San Angelo. You were in the Air Force at the time. From the first I was impressed with you. When things began taking shape for me to assume the full leadership of the church, and I began to analyze who I thought would make a great teammate, you were my first, and really, my only choice. You agreed to come and we worked together for at least a year before the full leadership transition took place.

As time went on I came to genuinely love you and respect you. While being different people with different personalities and gift sets (for instance, you're outgoing, I'm a recluse), we seemed to have the same philosophy of ministry and quickly learned to use our differences to forge a strong team. Back in those early days it was you, my wife, and me. We were the team. And I wouldn't have changed it for anything.

As time went by and the church grew and we added more staff, I think our relationship was viewed as special. We traveled quite a bit together, went to Friday night football games together (although you never stayed till the end), and though our families never hung out together much, our ministry experience forged a friendship that went way beyond the office or ministry. As I told you in an early email in this process, I would have taken a bullet for you.

I know that ministry peers envied the relationship we had. We enjoyed being around each other. The tough times seemed to make us stronger. I still think you and I were the best ministry team I have ever known."

The last time we sat in your office, it was clear that our relationship was ending. I remember we both said, "I hate that it's ending this way." That was devastating for both of us. For more than three years we didn't communicate even though we lived in the same town. God moved me to Southern California and moved you to Boston. About eight months ago, we agreed to give reconciliation a try. I was afraid of digging back into those painful memories and afraid of creating new ones. What did you dread most about entering this process?

"When we came to an impasse and I said, 'I think we're through,' and you walked out of my office, I felt like my world had suddenly stopped spinning on it axis. But it didn't stop there. I relived our split every day for years. I couldn't even think about it without bursting into tears.

If anyone who watched it thought there was a winner, they were wrong. The fallout was horrific at the church. People left the church. I lost my leadership integrity even with people who stayed, but viewed me with a suspicious eye for a long time after that. My greatest fear in life became running into you in public. I'm not going to lie; one of the happiest days of my life was the day I heard you had moved to California. That was a smattering of closure for me. At least the possibility of a chance meeting at Wal-Mart was behind me. Then we moved to Boston. Now we were on opposite sides of the nation. Even better yet!

And then I got your email. 'I don't even know what reconciliation would look like for us, but would you be willing to make the journey?' you wrote. I was surprised and scared, but I knew I had to try. If for no other reason, I was willing to take this journey for myself. The physical and emotional toll that unforgiveness and grudge-nursing had taken on me was horrific. So I said yes, if only for the hope of setting myself free.

The main thing I dreaded was rehashing everything. I knew that discussing those issues again would be brutal, and it was. But I felt like we labored until those feelings got lighter. It was the first time we had really talked (and listened) in several years."

You suggested limiting our interactions to email initially (which I think was wise for us). Initially, my heartbeat was so fast I thought it was going to explode as I nervously typed. Was it that emotionally charged for you?

"My heart was pounding so fast I needed oxygen. The emotion involved in this was almost overwhelming at first. I had two fears: 1) That I wouldn't be able to communicate what I needed to say; 2) I dreaded reading your responses. I figured one of us would say something that would ignite the whole thing over again. This didn't start because a couple of immature people got their feelings hurt and had a spat for which neither was willing to say, 'Sorry.' This was over real issues that we viewed differently, and then the fallout from it. For three years I thought, 'I can't believe he would do that to me,' and through our communication I discovered that for three years you had been saying, 'I can't believe he would do that to me.' Emotionally charged doesn't even begin to describe it. I was scared out of my mind."

We exchanged emails several times a week for a couple of months working through important issues. We didn't agree on everything, but I feel like we better understood each other's perspectives and were able to clarify some important details. Would you agree?

"What helped me the most was that early on there were apologies—on both sides. I think it indicated that our hearts were right in trying to heal deep wounds. I knew I had to get to the place that I could apologize, and I was willing to go there, but it helped immensely to know you were there also.

I knew early on in this process that we wouldn't see eye-to-eye on everything, but I also knew that if I was going to achieve any semblance of peace I had to get to the point that I was OK with that. I knew that neither of us could just say, 'Oops, sorry,' and sweep it all under the rug as if nothing had ever happened. We had to discuss some tough issues—the very ones that had divided us in the first place, and we had to get closure on them or this attempt would be a failure.

I thought that if we were going to take a stab at this we would need some pretty defined guidelines and boundaries. I thought we negotiated those well. It would take place via email (I couldn't have done this via phone. I wasn't there yet.) We also agreed that we would not allow reading anything into statements. It is impossible to read emotion or intent in an email, so if there were any uncertainties, we would stay at it until we got a clarification. Those happened several times. The other requirement had to be complete honesty.

I absolutely agree that we were able to clarify some important details. I think we both saw some statements and decisions that were made in a different light than before. I think we both came to understand several issues differently and gained insight and perspective that had been lost on us in the heat of the moment."

Reconciliation doesn't mean that everyone has to agree on everything. Here's some insight from one of your emails to me:

"I think there are things about those days that we would still disagree on and about, and I am perfectly OK with that. I have gotten some clarity and perspective through this quite extended exchange we have been having. My vote is that we move on and forward. We are both analytics and I suspect we could debate specific points till the cows come home, but my perspective is that would be pointless and potentially harmful, and I would like for our harmful days to be behind us. I would like for you and me to be able to do something that Paul and Barnabas were evidently unable to do: experience disagreement and hurt, but move past it to a restored friendship. The mutual regrets expressed, apologies offered, and explanations given are enough for me to move past them, and I am ready to do so."

The reconciliation process has helped me gain a bigger perspective about the past, about you, and about us, and softened my heart toward you. How has the reconciliation process helped you?

"In the same way. Although anything we build from here on out will obviously be built on the foundation of what we had before, I tend to see it more in the context of a new endeavor than a revival. We have common memories (and I think more good than bad), but everything else has changed. We live in different places. Our ministries are different. Our families are at different stages. That is a lot of new material with which to rebuild, with twelve years of great memories and victories thrown in to season it and give it a familiar foundation.

At the end of it all, I had to come to the place I was no longer willing to let one disagreement define my relationship with you. As stated, I'm sure we will never see everything about that issue eye-to-eye, but was I willing to let one issue kill the twelve incredible years we spent together in ministry? My answer was no. During those years we were leading the fastest growing church in San Angelo. Every day was a new adventure. We both wear wreathes and scars from those days and I wouldn't have wanted to have experienced that with anyone else. I wish we had not lost those years."

We are still rebuilding our friendship, and I can't tell you how grateful I am to have you back into my life. To

help display our renewed friendship, would you publicly and fully declare yourself a Dallas Cowboys' fan?

"Nope. That is where I draw the line. That loud thud you heard was me putting my foot down.

Q: What's the difference between the Dallas Cowboys and a dollar bill?

A: You can still get four quarters out of a dollar bill."

GET UNSTUCK: PUTTING IT TO WORK

Every time I re-read this interview, I smile. It still means a lot to me. So how about you? If appropriate, are you ready to reconcile?

1. If you're seeking an apology, then you're not ready to reconcile. Forgive first.

2. Establish that your goal is to simply be at peace with each other instead of trying to fully restore a friendship.

3. Seek to understand the other person's perspective. When you can paraphrase their thoughts back to them to their satisfaction, you know you're understanding them. Practice active listening.

4. Share your perspective without finger-pointing. Use "I" statements instead of "you" statements.

5. When possible, offer a regret or apology early in the process.

6. Discuss one issue at a time.

7. Don't read anything into the other person's statement. If you question something, ask about it.

8. Have someone you respect assist you through the process. I asked my wife and my Executive Pastor to "read and approve" each of my emails before sending them. I can't tell you how important this was for me!

Ten Forgiveness FAQs

1. How can I forgive myself?

Author R.T. Kendall wrote, "There is no lasting joy in forgiveness if it doesn't include forgiving yourself."

Identify the voice! Who's reminding you of your regret? God convicts you to change you. Satan condemns you to shame you. Reminder: confession and forgiveness do not eliminate consequences. Just because you're living with consequences as a result of your bad decisions does *not* mean you're *not* forgiven.

Distinguish between self-esteem and self-forgiveness. You esteem yourself for the good person you are. You forgive yourself for the bad things you did.

Honestly apologize to God *and* the offended party. As Lewis Smedes says, "Without honesty, self-forgiveness is psychological hocus-pocus. The rule is: we cannot really forgive ourselves unless we look at the failure in our past and call it by its right name."

Confess your regret to someone. We often over-condemn or gloss-over our past sin. Confessing our past sins helps us see a healthier perspective. "Therefore confess your sins to each other and pray for each other so that you may be healed. The prayer of a righteous person is powerful and effective" (James 5:16).

Complete the same six-step forgiveness process outlined in this book (S.A.V.I.O.R.) forgiving yourself as the offender.

With your newly forgiven heart, perform a reckless act of love. "We love because we have been forgiven much" (Luke 7:47). Your love seals your forgiveness.

2. How can I forgive God?

R.T. Kendall's words help here too: "Although we often do not see it at first—and for some it takes a long time—all of our bitterness is ultimately traceable to a resentment of God. This may be an unconscious anger. Why do we feel this way? Because deep in our hearts we believe that He is the one who allowed bad things to happen in our lives. Since He is all-powerful and all-knowing, couldn't He have prevented tragedies and offenses from happening? He has allowed us to suffer when we didn't do anything, or so it seems, to warrant such ill treatment. What we ultimately believe is that God is to blame for our hurt."

To forgive God is to release him from blame for the injustices you've experienced. This is a temporary measure that may be necessary to allow you to move toward God in trust. When you know what God knows, you will see that his ways are right and your forgiveness was not called for—but still granted.

In the meantime, cling to two truths:

"The LORD is close to the brokenhearted and saves those who are crushed in spirit" (Psalm 34:18).

"And we know that in all things God works for the good of those who love him, who have been called according to his purpose" (Romans 8:28).

3. Why does forgiveness feel so messy?

We are humans entering divine behavior. Forgiveness isn't a clean, scientific process. Lewis Smedes says it quite visually: "We will always be mucking our way through grace." And C.S. Lewis warns people away from the faith on account of its high demands: "If you want a religion to make you feel really comfortable, I certainly don't recommend Christianity." Forgiveness is a beautifully messy process that makes God smile every time you try.

4. How can I forgive if they have not apologized?

Withholding forgiveness until your offender apologizes puts your offender in charge of your forgiveness. Forgiveness is always for people who don't deserve it. Grace that's earned isn't grace. There is a difference between forgiveness given and forgiveness received. We're only responsible for forgiveness given, not forgiveness received.

5. How long will it take me to forgive?

Slowly, and longer than you want. People are unique and each situation is unique, so it's impossible to predict a timeframe. The general rule is: the deeper the hurt, the longer the process.

Forgiveness is usually a cycle, which we need to repeat in order to sustain it. My observation is that fast forgiveness fades. Some people, myself included, try to forgive quickly after experiencing a deep hurt in an attempt to avoid pain. Forgiveness is a difficult but worthwhile process. It is rarely fast and often needs a second coat.

6. Can I forgive someone who's still hurting me?

Jesus forgave on the cross while his offenders still mocked him from below. God's grace is always greater. However, forgiving someone who's still hurting you may be the hardest assignment of all. Nelson Mandela said we don't forgive "while the boot is still on our neck."

You do not need to allow them to hurt you or to continue taking advantage of you. You do not have to stay with them or even have a relationship with them.

7. How often should I forgive them?

Infinitely.

We do not have to tolerate, excuse, or diminish their actions, but we should offer limitless forgiveness. That was Jesus' point in Matthew 18 when he told Peter to forgive seventy times seven.

In other words, there's no limit.

8. Should I tell the person I've forgiven them?

In many cases, silent forgiveness is better than spoken forgiveness. People who hurt us may not realize it, may not agree with our interpretation, may not be alive, or may not care. In many cases, a conversation would only worsen the situation. Lewis Smedes says that "Forgiving is essential; talking about it is optional."

9. If my anger towards them returns, does that mean I didn't forgiven them?

If forgiveness is the hardest thing God ever asks you to do, expect relapses. Remember, emotions are great indicators, but terrible leaders. Surrender your emotions (anger) to God. Then choose to lead your emotions. Again, Lewis Smedes wryly writes, "Forgiving is the hardest chord to play in the human concerto."

10. Am I supposed to forgive *and* forget?

Desmond Tutu said that "Forgiving is not forgetting; it's actually remembering—remembering and not using your right to hit back. It's a second chance for a new beginning. And the remembering part is particularly important. Especially if you don't want to repeat what happened."

You can forgive, but you will still remember. Smedes said, "A healed memory is not a deleted memory." Remembering healed pain can be a positive connection with the past. When Satan brings the pain to your mind, forgiveness allows you to say, "Yes, I remember specifically forgiving *and* overcoming that."

About the Author

Mark Riggins grew up in Texas and served in the U.S. Air Force prior to entering full-time ministry.

Mark is the Community Life Pastor for ENCOUNTER at Bible Fellowship Church in Ventura, CA. Before that, he was the Lead Pastor of a church plant with North Point Ministries. Mark holds a Master's degree from Liberty Theological Seminary.

ABOUT THE AUTHOR

Mark and his wife Ginger have four children: Reagen, Kennedy, Lincoln, and Madison, and a Labrador named Malibu, a.k.a. "Mali."

Follow Mark on Twitter @markriggins or connect through his blog at www.markriggins.org.

ENDNOTES

1   Adapted with permission from Pastor Mark Driscoll's "Ten Things Forgiveness is Not."

2   Copyright 2012 by Robert D. Enright. Reproduced with permission. The Forgiving Life (APA Lifetools) (Kindle Location 2066-2067). EXHIBIT 8.2. Definitions of Categories for Describing Each Incident of Injustice, American Psychological Association.

3   Chip Dodd, The Voice of the Heart: A Call to Full Living. (Nashville: Sage Hill Resources, 2001), 31.

4   Lewis Smedes, Forgive & Forget: Healing the Hurts We Don't Deserve (San Francisco, Harper & Row, 1984), xiii-xv.

5   Story adapted with permission from Woody Woodburn (www.woodywoodburn.com).

Made in the USA
San Bernardino, CA
09 July 2018